KU-618-720

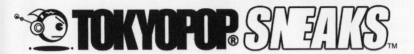

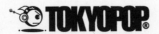

HAMBURG // LONDON // LOS ANGELES // TOKYO

# Introduction

Welcome to the latest installment of TOKYOPOP Sneaks, your insider's guide to the wild and wonderful world of manga!

As you may already know, manga – the Japanese word for comics– has become a truly global phenomenon. All over the world, readers can't get enough of its irresistible visual storytelling and bleeding-edge graphic design. There's manga for every taste, too: science fiction, romance, comedy, fantasy, action...you name it and TOKYOPOP has it covered!

Within the pages of this book, you will find an extraordinary selection of TOKYOPOP's latest titles that are sure to fire your imagination like nothing you have ever read before. Once you pick out your favorites, remember that TOKYOPOP manga is available everywhere books are sold.

Check your local bookstore, go to your favorite e-commerce site, or visit TOKYOPOP's online shop at www.TOKYOPOP.co.uk to buy the latest and greatest TOKYOPOP manga.

From all of us here at TOKYOPOP, thank you for your support – and welcome to the Manga Revolution!

# TOKYOPOP® SNEAKS™

left to right ———▶ left to right ———▶ left to right ——

## TABLE OF CONTENTS

## The Story:

So-jin had given up soccer years ago after losing to her rival, Shin-bee. But when she transfers into a co-ed high school, the football bug returns, and she challenges the boys to a soccer tournament!

## The Creator:

Jae-ho Youn

ACTION

T

TEEN
AGE 13+

## SRP:

£6.99

YOU PIECE OF TRASH!

I NEVER ONCE THOUGHT OF YOU AS FAMILY.

GRANDPA'S GETTING HIS WISH!

HEH. SO I HEARD.

"THOSE WHO CAN, DO." SINCE YOU'RE A TEACHER...

WE'LL FIND OUT GRAMP'S TRUE INTENTIONS FOR HIS ASSETS.

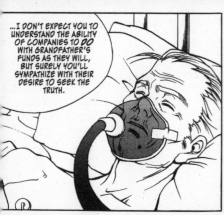

...I DON'T EXPECT YOU TO UNDERSTAND THE ABILITY OF COMPANIES TO DO WITH GRANDFATHER'S FUNDS AS THEY WILL, BUT SURELY YOU'LL SYMPATHIZE WITH THEIR DESIRE TO SEEK THE TRUTH.

I THINK IT'LL BE A VERY SHORT SEARCH, "COUSIN." AND OH, I DON'T THINK OF YOU AS FAMILY EITHER.

HA HA HA HA!!

CHAE-YOUNG, DON'T BE UPSET.

OKAY...

MY BROTHER WAS BECOMING AN OLD, OLD MAN...

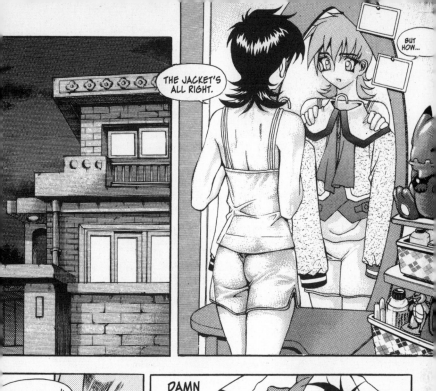

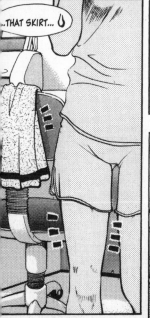

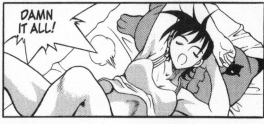

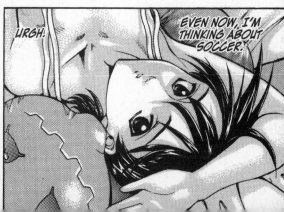

ACCORDING TO HIS WILL, CHAIRMAN YOON WILL BE DONATING FIFTY PERCENT OF HIS ASSETS TO THE KOREAN SOCCER ASSOCIATION IN ORDER TO DEVELOP A WOMEN'S SOCCER LEAGUE.

THE SOCCER ASSOCIATION EXPRESSED GRATITUDE AND SAID THAT CHAIRMAN YOON'S DONATION WILL BE AN IMPORTANT STEPPING STONE FOR WOMEN'S SOCCER IN KOREA.

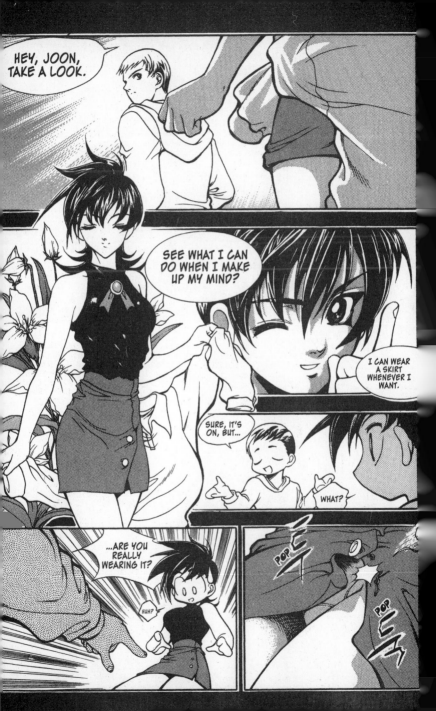

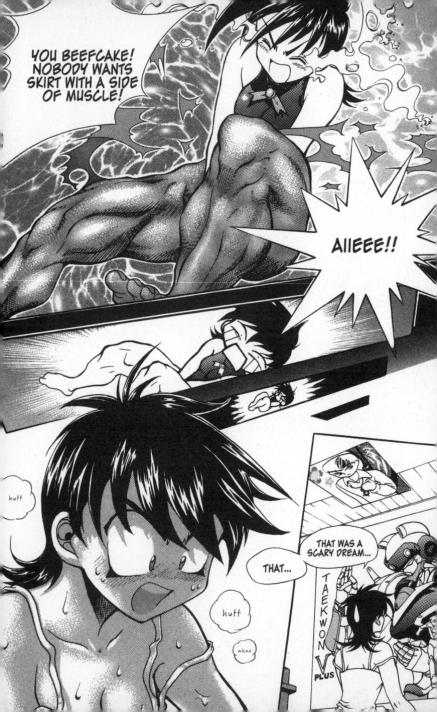

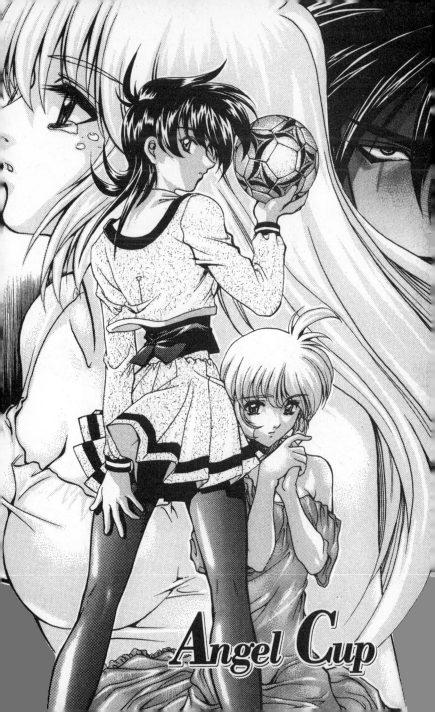

Angel Cup

WOO-JIN! WAKE UP YOUR SISTER!

The Grand Opening of Dad's Dental Office

Big Brother Woo-jin

YAH, SURE.

LET'S NOT BE LATE FOR OUR FIRST DAY, SO-JIN!

NEITHER YOU NOR ME!

JEEZ...

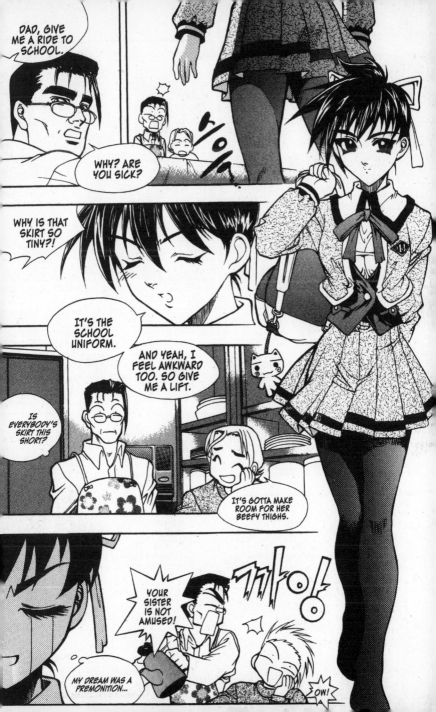

YOU LOOK FINE, SWEETIE.

YOU'RE JUST AS BEAUTIFUL AS YOUR MOTHER. SHE WOULD BE SO PROUD OF YOU NOW.

HA!

THANKS.

FOR SHAME, DAD. I'M THE ONE WHO GOT THE LOOKS OUTTA THIS BUNCH.

YOU'LL NEED THOSE LOOKS, SEEING AS NO COLLEGE HAS ACCEPTED YOU.

AH!

OH, YOU THINK A LITTLE THING LIKE NOT HAVING A COLLEGE EDUCATION WILL KEEP ME FROM ACHIEVING IN LIFE?!

SHE'S RIGHT, SON.

DAAAAD!

AHH! LOOK AT THE TIME! WE'LL BE LATE! HURRY UP!!

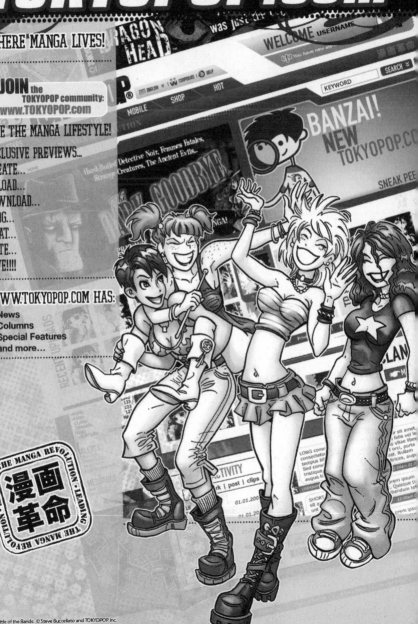
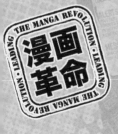

## The Story:

When a group of seven young college students go off to enjoy a weekend getaway at a remote mountain villa, secrets that haunt the friends are unveiled...which lead to bizarre love triangles, tragic relationships, and betrayal. And when hallucinations and strange disappearances begin, their dream vacation turns into a nightmare...

## The Creator:

Ya-Seong Ko

HORROR

OT
OLDER TEEN
AGE 16+

## SRP:

£6.99

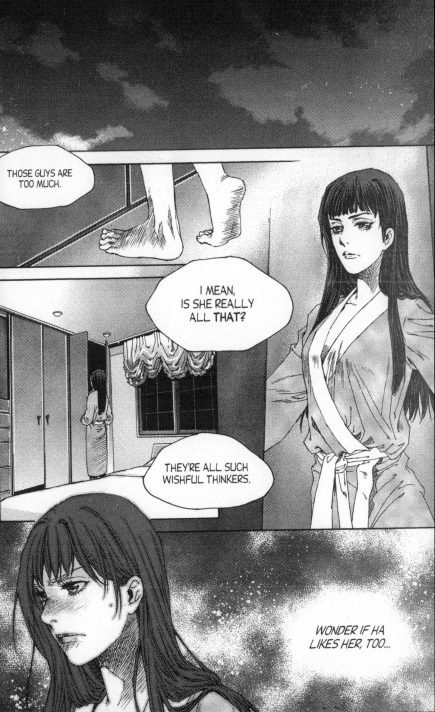

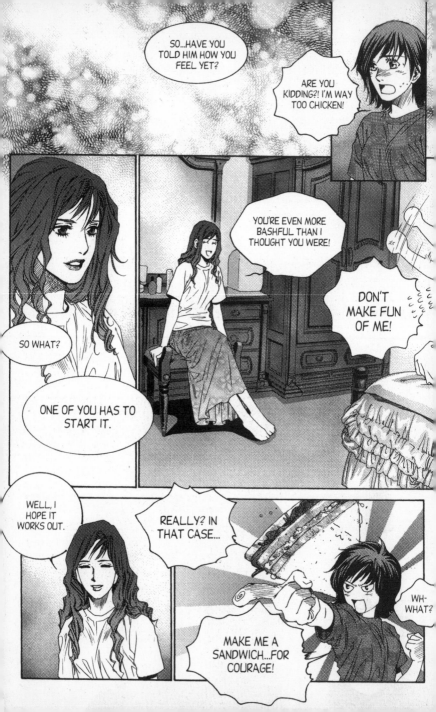

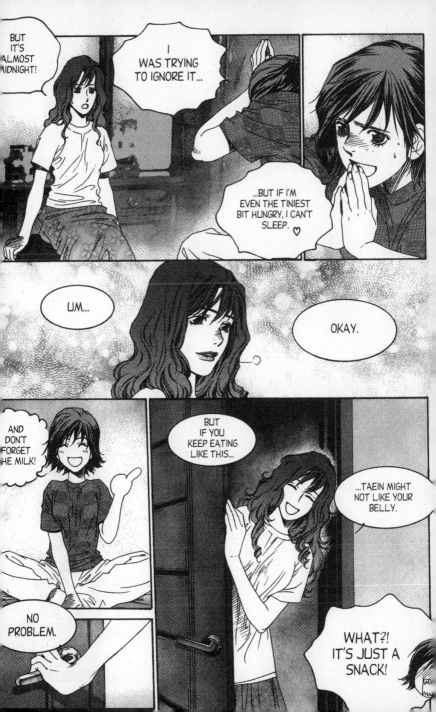

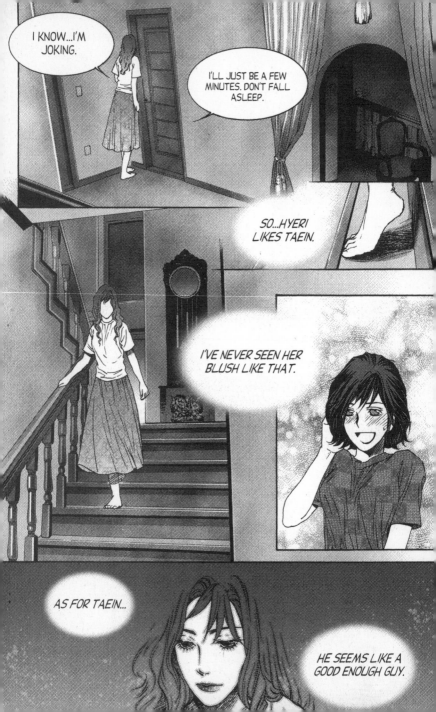

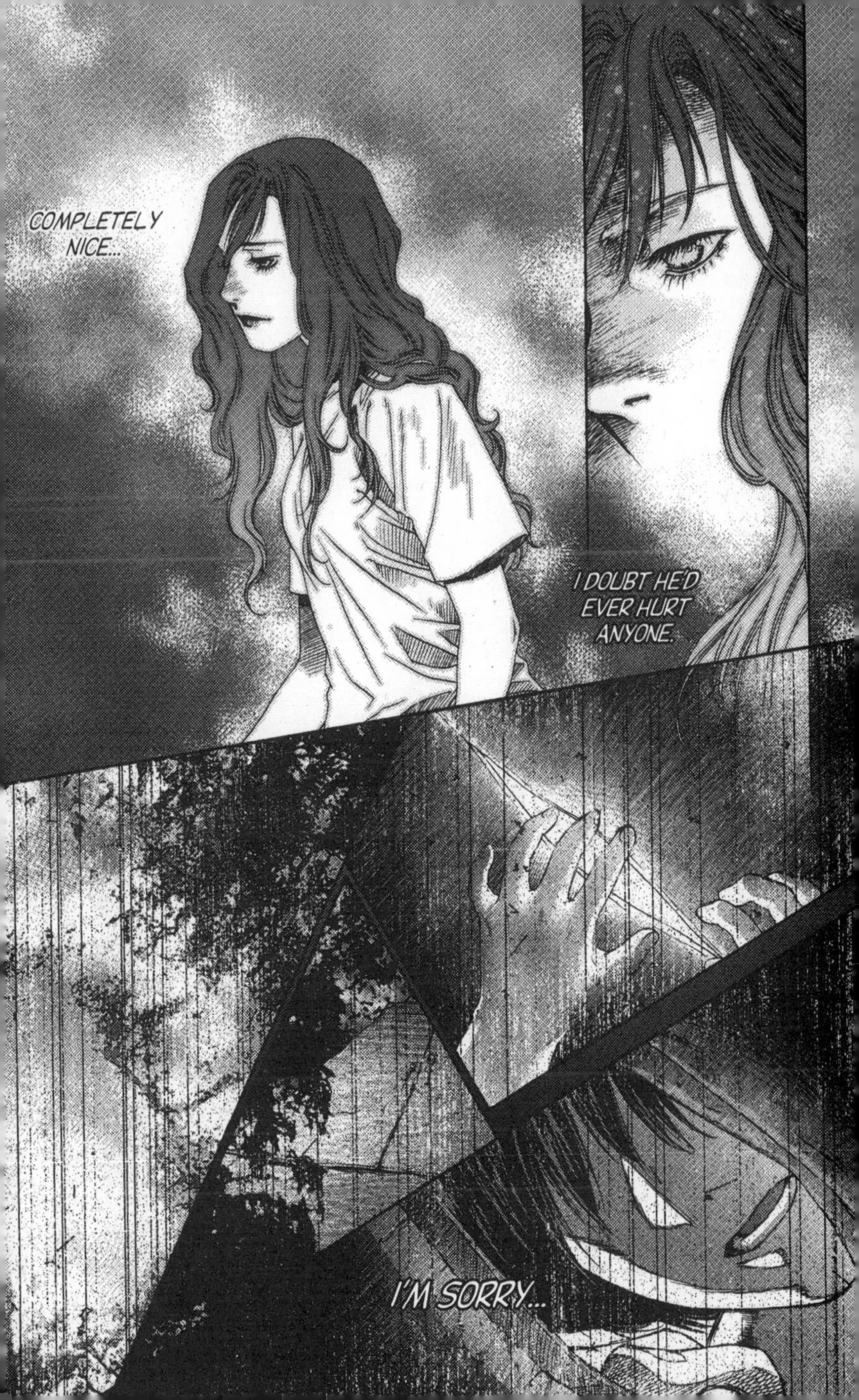
COMPLETELY NICE...
I DOUBT HE'D EVER HURT ANYONE.
I'M SORRY...

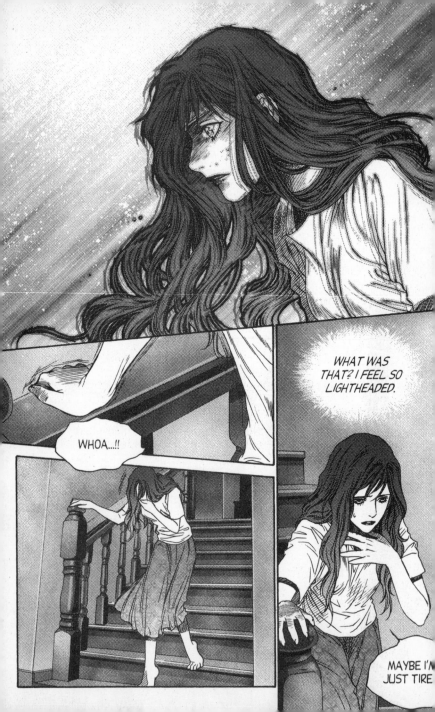

NO. I'M NOT LOSING MY MIND AGAIN.

GOT TO KEEP IT TOGETHER...

AH, THAT HYERI...

...ALWAYS THINKING ABOUT FOOD.

IT'S TRUE, THOUGH. GIRLS BECOME SO MUCH MORE ATTRACTIVE WHEN THEY FALL—

CRUMPLE...

?!

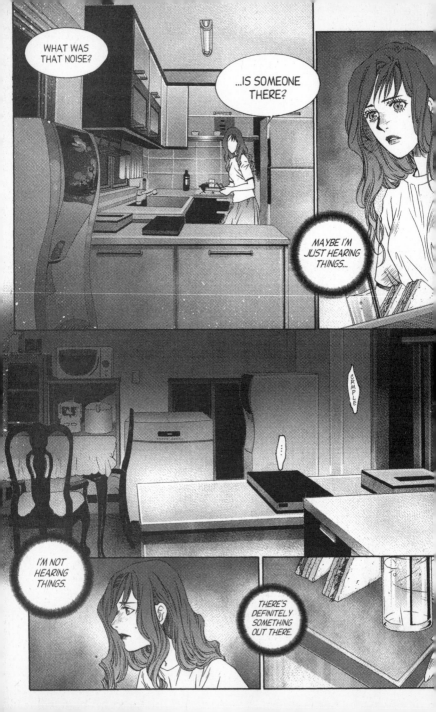

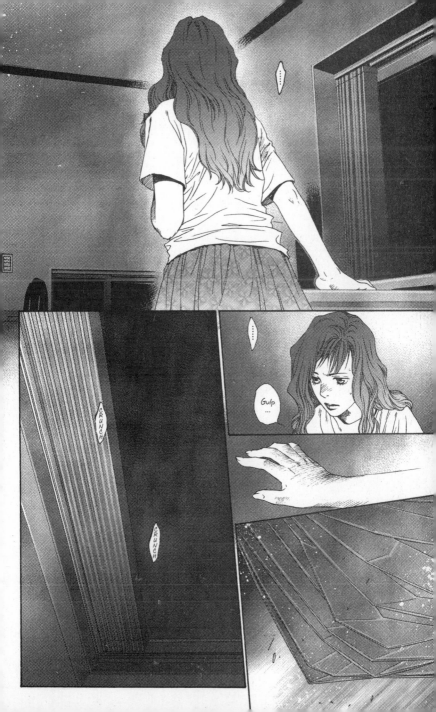

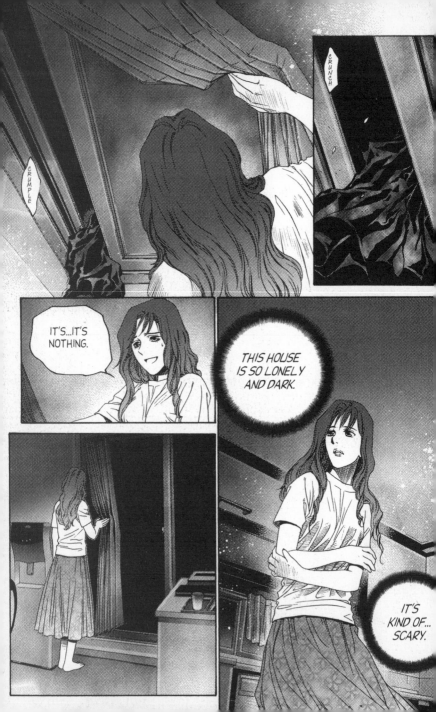

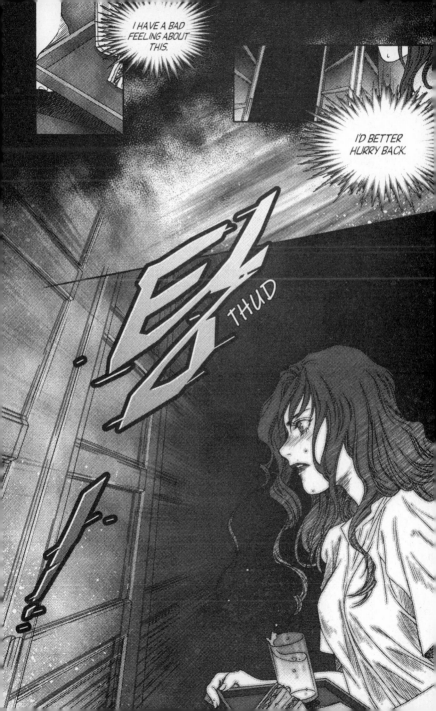

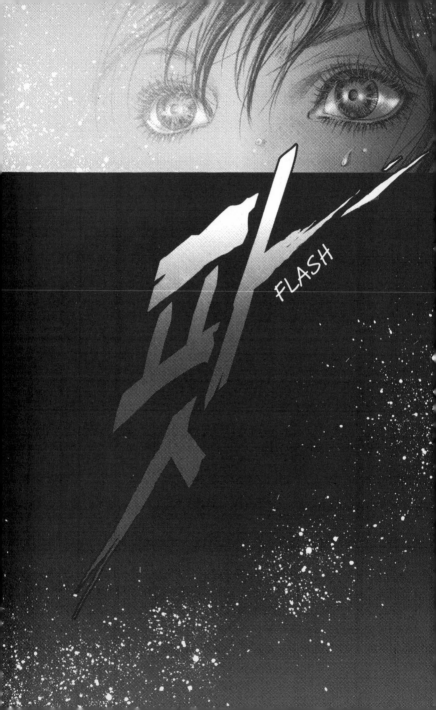
FLASH

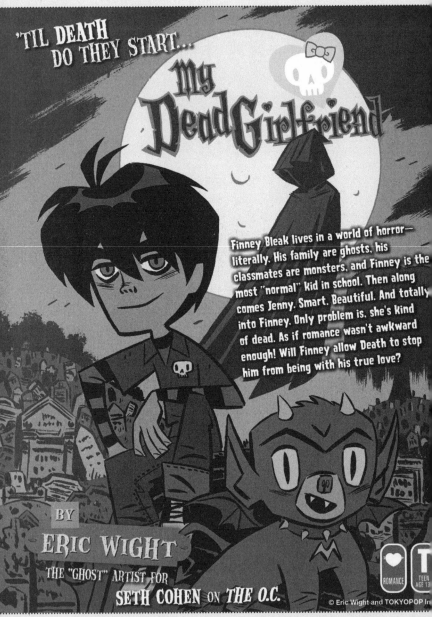

# CHECK INTO MYSTERY.

MYSTERIOUS CASE AT HOTEL DUSK.

24 DECEMBER 1976 NEW YORK.

BRADLEY?!

THE BODY IS MISSING...

SHOT!?

WHY?

WHAT HAPPENED THAT NIGHT?

Kyle Hyde

SHE KNOWS BRADLEY?

HOTEL DUSK
Room 215.

HOTEL DUSK

HOTEL DUSK
Room 215

NINTENDO DS lite

Check in for a night of mystery and intrigue at Hotel Dusk. Will you solve the series of complex puzzles to discover what is really going on in Room 215? Unravel the secrets of Kyle Hyde's past to reveal the truth behind the events of that dark night in '76 in this interactive mystery thriller for Nintendo DS.

# S⋄RCERERS
## SECRETARIES

### The Story:

Nicole Hayes sure likes to daydream--and who can blame her? She studies a subject she has no interest in so she can satisfy her mother, and she works part time as a receptionist to satisfy her bills. But when she's alone with her notebook, she crafts a fantastic story and lets her imagination go-go-go! Meanwhile, her old neighbor Josh Kim pines after her every step but just can't seem to snap her out of her daydreams and get her to notice him. If only he could see what she's dreaming about, maybe he could finally win her over.

### The Creator:

Amy Kim Ganter

### SRP:

£6.99

Far away in another realm there lives a sorcerer named Ellon, and his familiar, Sonneth.

With his piles of precious stones, Ellon bides his time conjuring kind and just leaders for the realm of humanity by carving magical statues that bring them into being.

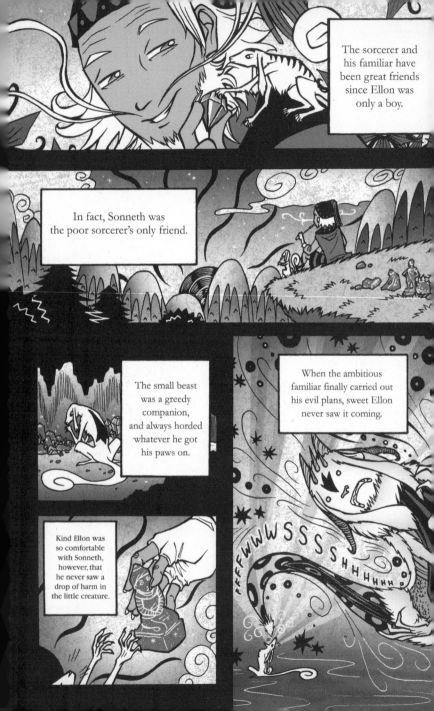

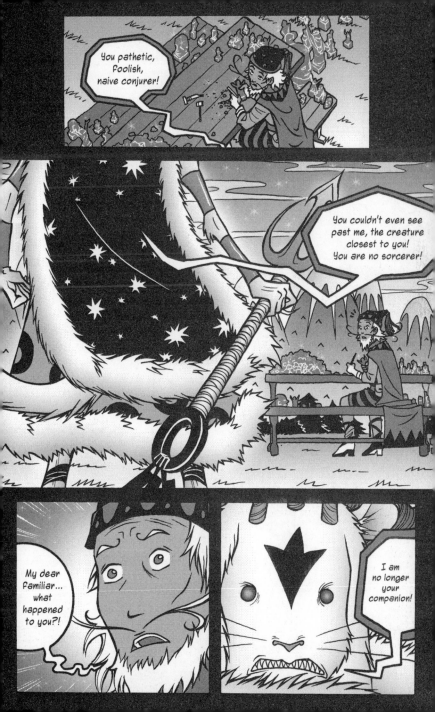

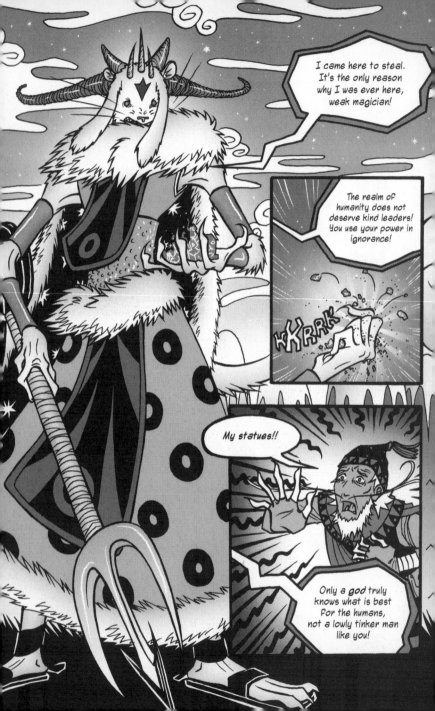

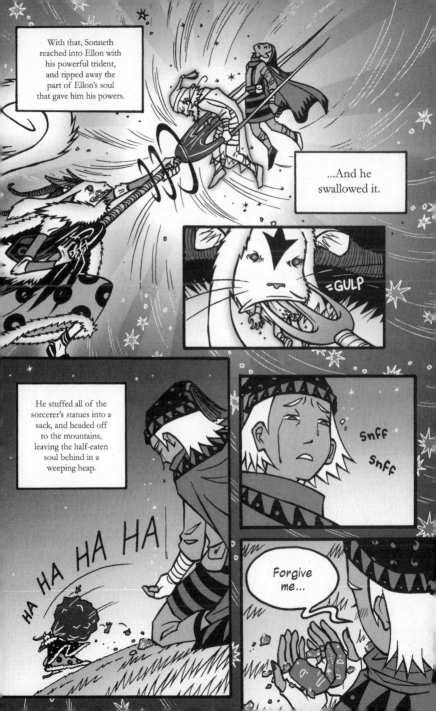

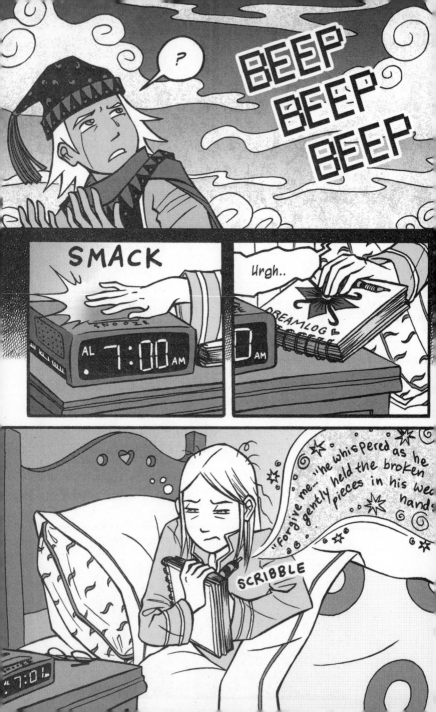

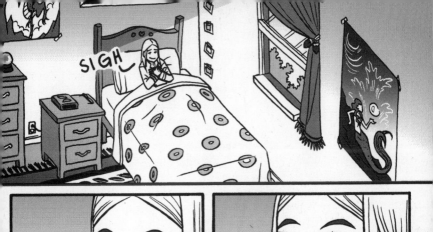

SIGH

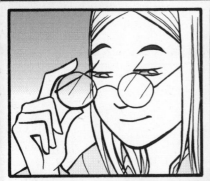

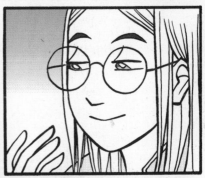

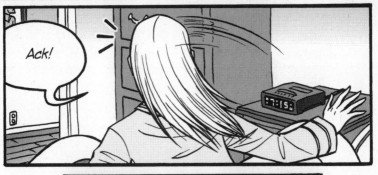

Ack!

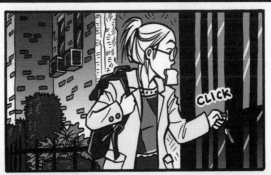

CLICK

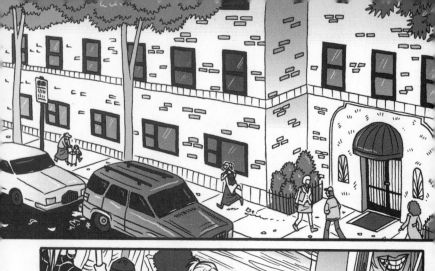

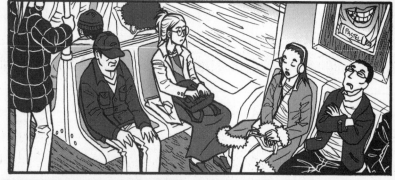

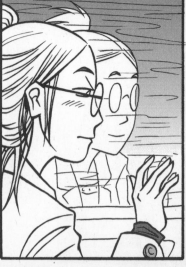

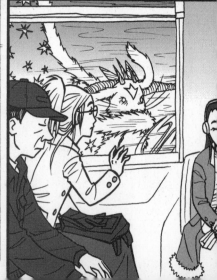

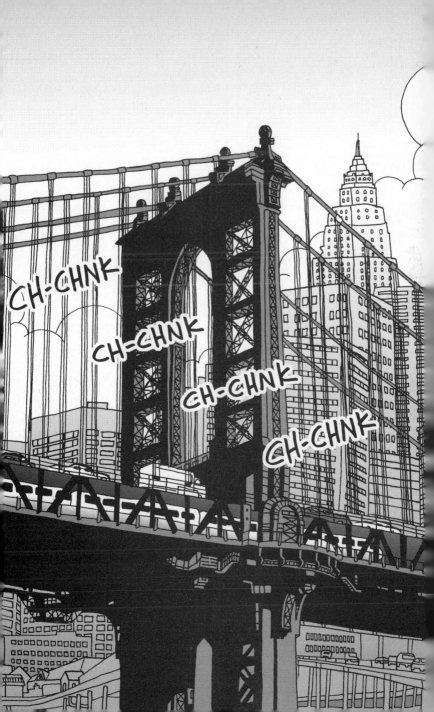

Speaking of which, the test last week was a breeze for most of you, minus a few stragglers.

...And that concludes our study on Dynamic Pricing Rivalry.

What to do now that his power was gone? Did he even deserve to live in the Sacred Realm any longer? The sorcerer wept in his despair

You can do better.

=SIGH=

I just bought this shirt, and I saw Allison Stiles wearing it on the way here. Now I have to return it!

I mean, what if we show up in the same class one day and we're both wearing the same thing? That would be sooo embarassing!

But I guess this is what happens when I buy things I saw in *Girlfriend! Magazine*, huh?

=POOMF=

. . .

Were you even listening to anything I just said?

You bought a shirt that you saw in *Girlfriend!* Magazine and Allison Stiles bought the same one and you want to return it because you don't want to show up in class wearing the same thing.

What's that you're working on, Snickers?

Nothing.

C'mooon, what is it? Is it love letters?

No.

Omigod, it's not a diary, is it?!

It's private, I'd rather not talk about it.

Oh, all right.

Well, I'd better head out to JOG.

They're starting a billboard campaign for that clothing company, Snap Lush!

You workin' today, right?

Yup.

Sah-weet! See ya there, Snickers!

## The Story:

It's the year 2504. In the aftermath of an apocalyptic war, the surviving humans are ruled by the Beasterians, animal-human hybrids created to be the ultimate soldiers, but who instead became merciless tyrants. Doomed to extinction, humanity's future rests with the savior whose birth is foretold by the Post-Testament Bible.

From the creative mind of famed artist Jae-Hwan Kim (*King of Hell* and *Warcraft: The Sunwell Trilogy*) comes the story of the War Angels: the super-powered warriors who fight to protect humanity's last hope!

## The Creator:

Jae-Hwan Kim

ACTION

OT
OLDER TEEN
AGE 16+

## SRP:

£6.99

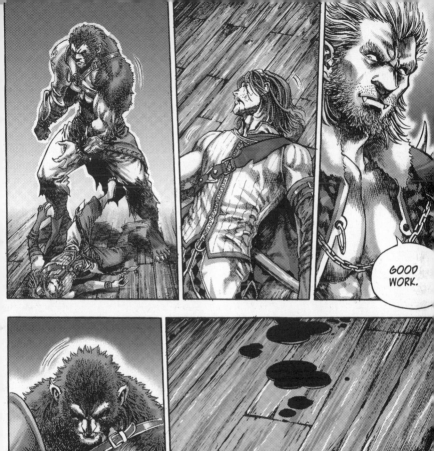

GOOD
WORK.

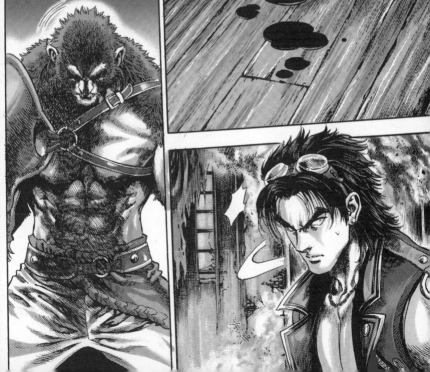

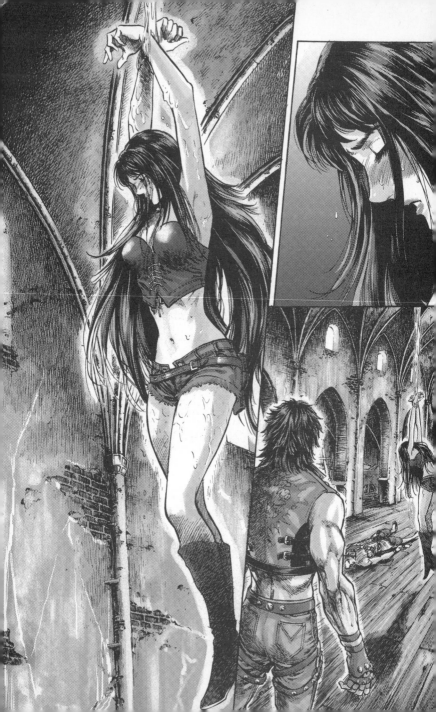

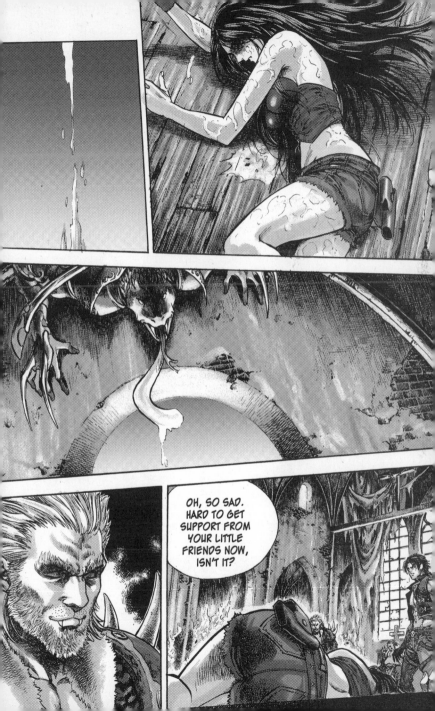

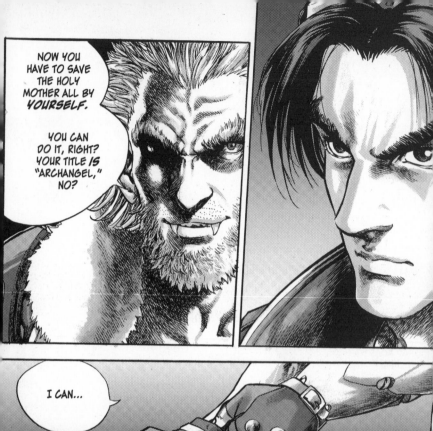

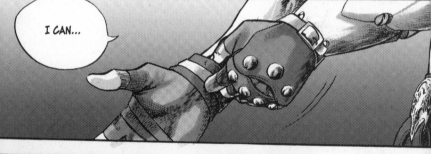

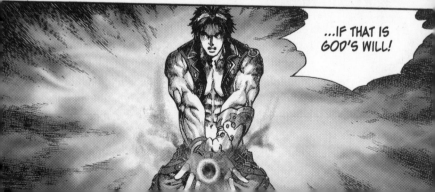

YOU MUSTN'T!

!!

DON'T STAND AGAINST HIM!

EVERYONE... EVERYONE WILL DIE!

HE WILL DESTROY EVERYTHING!

HOLY MOTHER!

WE ANGELS HAVE BEEN CHARGED TO *STOP* THAT DESTRUCTION!!

THAT IS WHY YOU MUST SURVIVE...

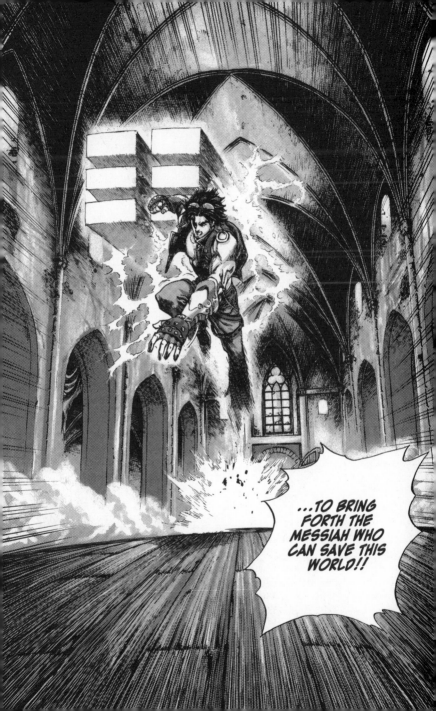

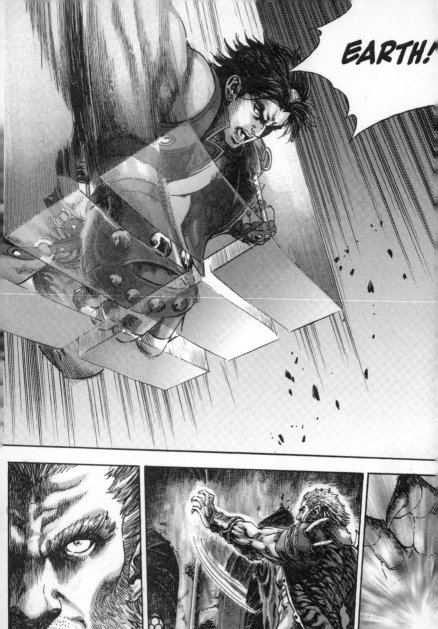

EARTH!

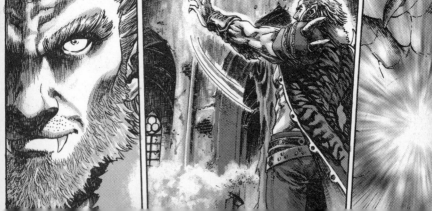

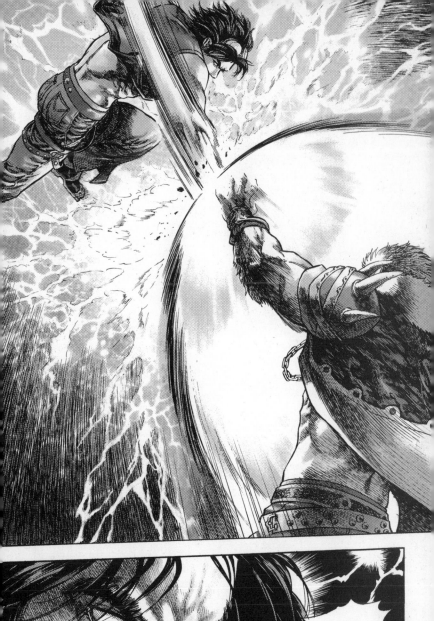
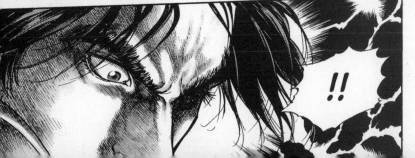

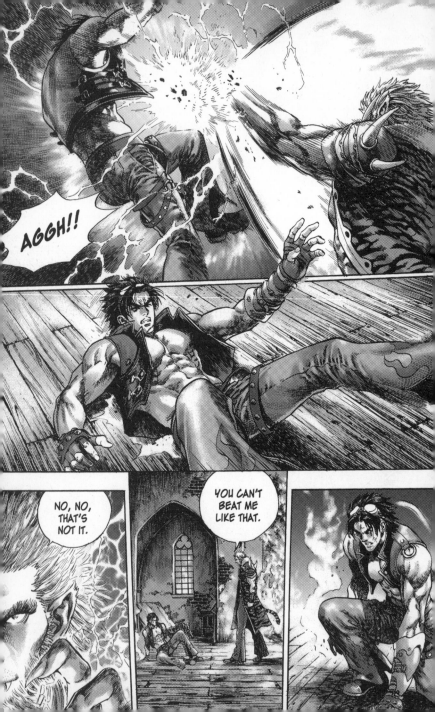

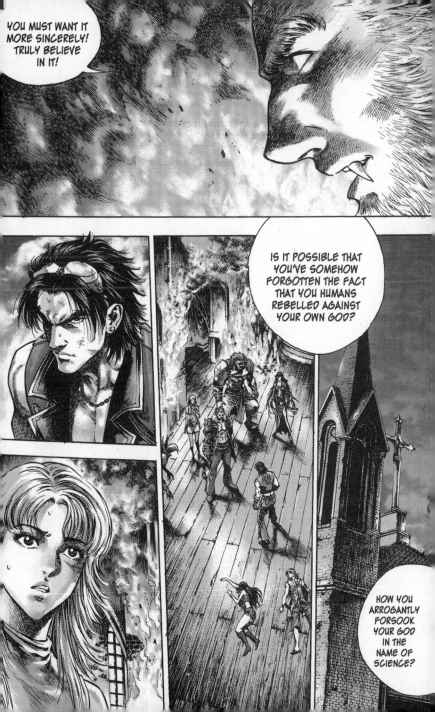

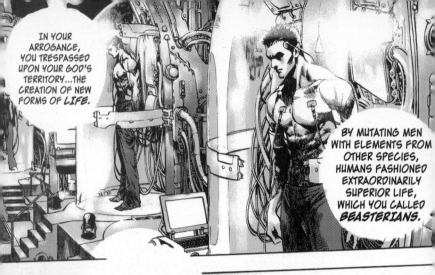

IN YOUR ARROGANCE, YOU TRESPASSED UPON YOUR GOD'S TERRITORY...THE CREATION OF NEW FORMS OF *LIFE.*

BY MUTATING MEN WITH ELEMENTS FROM OTHER SPECIES, HUMANS FASHIONED EXTRAORDINARILY SUPERIOR LIFE, WHICH YOU CALLED *BEASTERIANS.*

LIFE CREATED TO BE SACRIFICED IN WARS CAUSED BY YOUR *DIRTY DESIRES!*

EVENTUALLY, YOUR GOD COULD TOLERATE THIS WICKEDNESS NO FURTHER, AND PASSED A JUDGMENT... *THE JUDGMENT OF FIRE!*

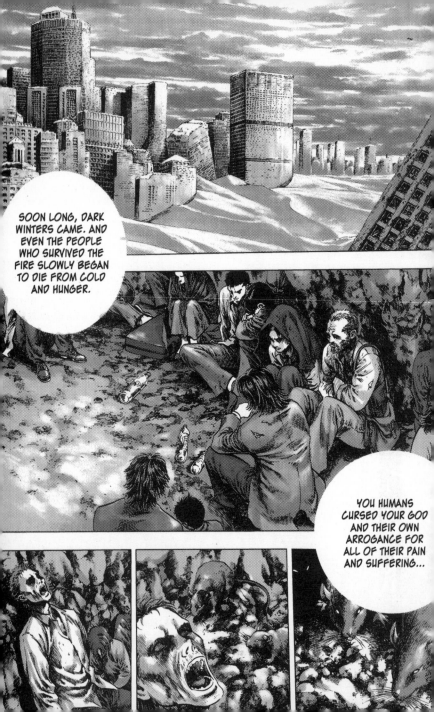

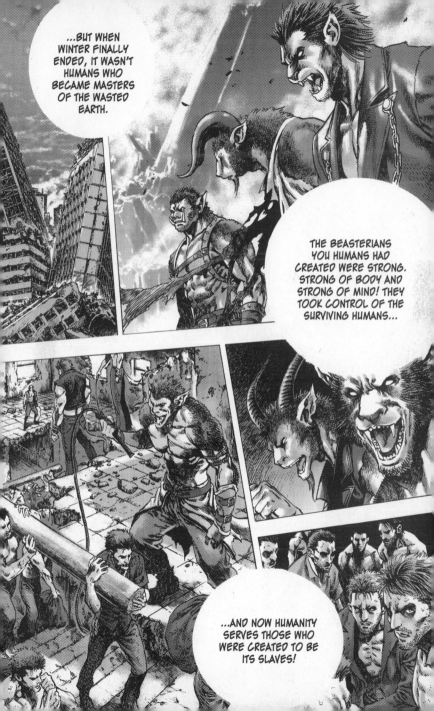

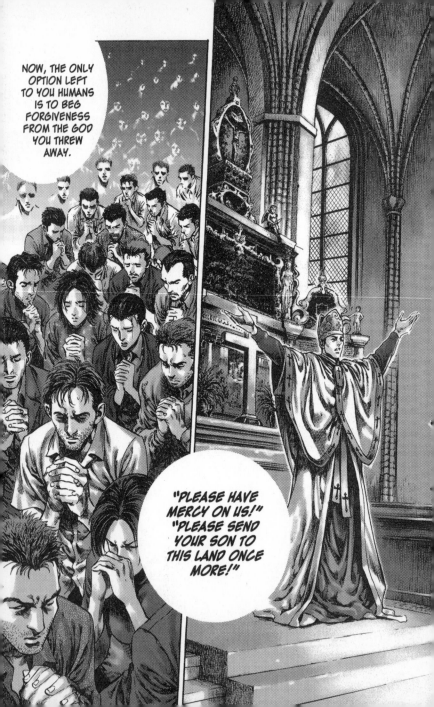

IS THIS THE SUM TOTAL OF HUMAN FAITH? TO ONLY BELIEVE WHEN THERE IS NO OTHER OPTION?

HA HA HA HA! PATHETIC! EVEN AFTER ALL YOU'VE SUFFERED...

...YOU STILL DON'T WANT SALVATION BADLY ENOUGH!

DAMN YOU...!

ALL RIGHT, HOW ABOUT SOMETHING LIKE THIS?

BEHOLD:

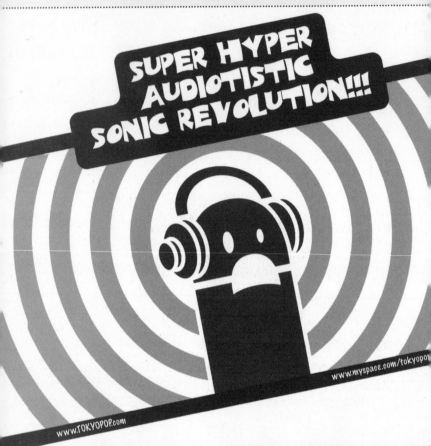

WE INTERRUPT THE MANGA TO BRING YOU THIS VERY IMPORTANT ANNOUNCEMENT:

# PauSE

## read right-to-left

If you've been enjoying the unforgettable left-to-right reading experience, we invite you to jump to the back of our manga sampler for more cutting-edge manga...this time from Japan!

## read left-to-right

If you've just soaked up the hottest manga from Japan, you need to turn to the front of our manga sampler for some of TOKYOPOP's originally created manga and other cool articles.

Of course, if you're blown away by what you've been reading, then e-mail your friends, call your loved ones, and write the president—tell them all about the Manga Revolution!

And make sure you log on to www.TOKYOPOP.com for more manga!

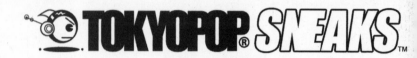

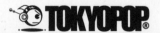

HAMBURG // LONDON // LOS ANGELES // TOKYO

# Introduction

Welcome to the latest installment of TOKYOPOP Sneaks, your insider's guide to the wild and wonderful world of manga!

As you may already know, manga – the Japanese word for comics– has become a truly global phenomenon. All over the world, readers can't get enough of its irresistible visual storytelling and bleeding-edge graphic design. There's manga for every taste, too: science fiction, romance, comedy, fantasy, action...you name it and TOKYOPOP has it covered!

Within the pages of this book, you will find an extraordinary selection of TOKYOPOP's latest titles that are sure to fire your imagination like nothing you have ever read before. Once you pick out your favorites, remember that TOKYOPOP manga is available everywhere books are sold.

Check your local bookstore, go to your favorite e-commerce site, or visit TOKYOPOP's online shop at www.TOKYOPOP.co.uk to buy the latest and greatest TOKYOPOP manga.

From all of us here at TOKYOPOP, thank you for your support – and welcome to the Manga Revolution!

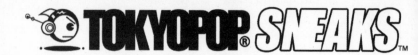

## TABLE OF CONTENTS

TOKYOPOP Sneaks UK 2007 vol. 2
Cover Art – Christopher Tjalsma
Graphic Design – Skooter
Project Coordinators – Kasia Piekarz and Rob Tokar
Digital Imaging Manager – Chris Buford
Pre-Press Manager – Erika Terriquez
Production Manager – Elisabeth Brizzi
Managing Editor – Vy Ngyuen
Creative Director – Anne Marie Horne
Editor-in-Chief – Rob Tokar
Publisher – Mike Kiley
President & C.O.O. – John Parker
C.E.O. & Chief Creative Officer – Stuart Levy

A  Manga

TOKYOPOP and 🐱 are trademarks or registered trademarks of TOKYOPOP Inc.

TOKYOPOP Inc.
5900 Wilshire Blvd. Suite 2000
Los Angeles, CA 90036
E-mail: info@TOKYOPOP.com
Come visit us online at www.TOKYOPOP.com
http://www.tokyopop.co.uk/

Angel Cup
© JAE-HO YOUN, AI, DAIWON C.I. Inc.

Beyond the Beyond
© YOSHITOMO WATANABE / MAG Garden

Bloodsucker
© AKI SHIMIZU / SAKI OKUSE

Bus Gamer 1999-2001 The Pilot Edition
© 2003 Kazuya Minekura / ICHIJINSHA

Dazzle
© Minari Endoh / ICHIJINSHA

Gothic Sports
© Anike Hage / TOKYOPOP GmbH. All rights reserved.

Good Witch of the West
© NORIKO OGIWARA / HARUHIKO MOMOKAWA / MAG Garden

King of Thorn
© YUJI IWAHARA

Redrum 327
© YA-SEONG KO, DAIWON C.I. Inc.

Sorcerers and Secretaries
© Amy Kim Ganter and TOKYOPOP Inc.

tactics
© SAKURA KINOSHITA and KAZUKO HIGASHIYAMA / MAG Garden

War Angels
© Jae-Hwan Kim and TOKYOPOP Inc.

English text copyright © 2007 TOKYOPOP Inc.
TOKYOPOP Sneaks is published for promotional use only.

ISBN: 978-1-4278-0508-9

First TOKYOPOP printing: October 2007

Printed in Germany

# 🌀 TOKYOPOP® SNEAKS™

## RIGHT-TO-LEFT CHEAT SHEET

This book is printed "manga-style," in the authentic Japanese right-to-l
format. Since none of the artwork has been flipped or altered, readers
get to experience the story just as the creator intended. You've been
asking for it, so TOKYOPOP® delivered: authentic, hot-off-the-press,
and far more fun!

# DIRECTIONS

If this is your first time
reading manga-style, here's a
quick guide to help you
understand how it works.

It's easy... just start in the top
right panel and follow the
numbers. Have fun, and look fo
more 100% authentic manga
from TOKYOPOP®!

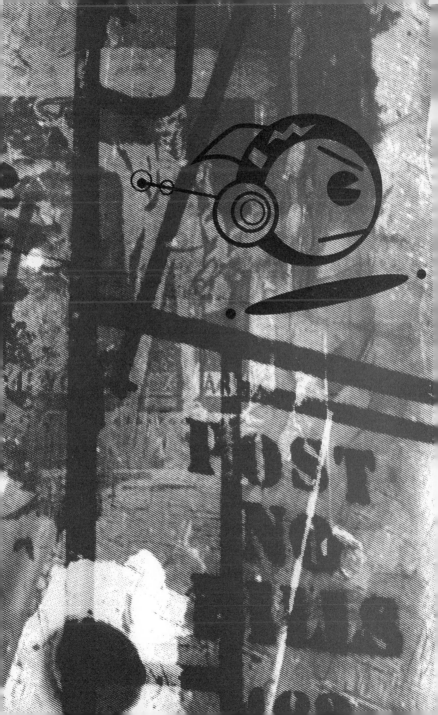

## The Story:

Futaba, a boy who has grown up in an overprotected family, suddenly finds himself on the other side of the world, where he meets Kiara, the Amaranthine. They journey to find Kiara's true master, and along the way they meet a curious cast of characters, including the wizard Belbel and the prince Vidit. Once Kiara finds her true master, Futaba hopes that they can open the gate that will allow him to get back to his side of the world!

## The Creator:

Yoshitomo Watanabe

FANTASY

T
TEEN
AGE 13+

## SRP:

£6.99

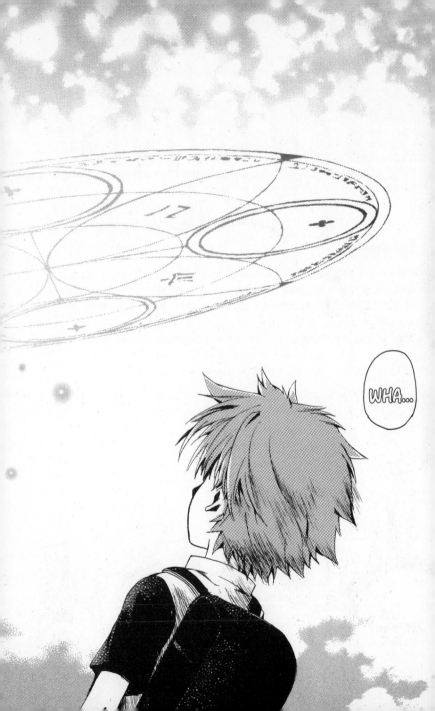

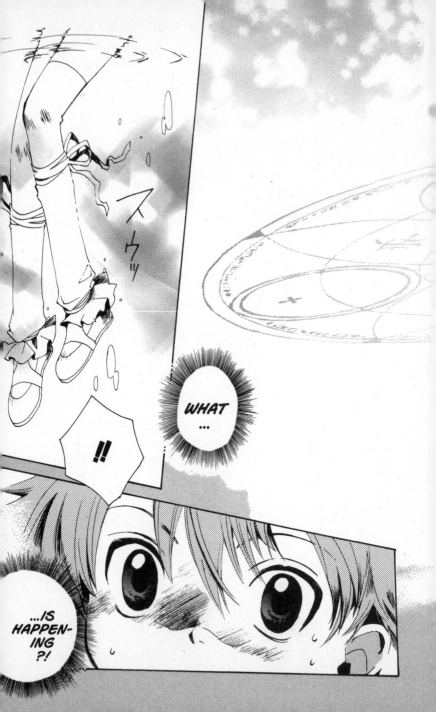

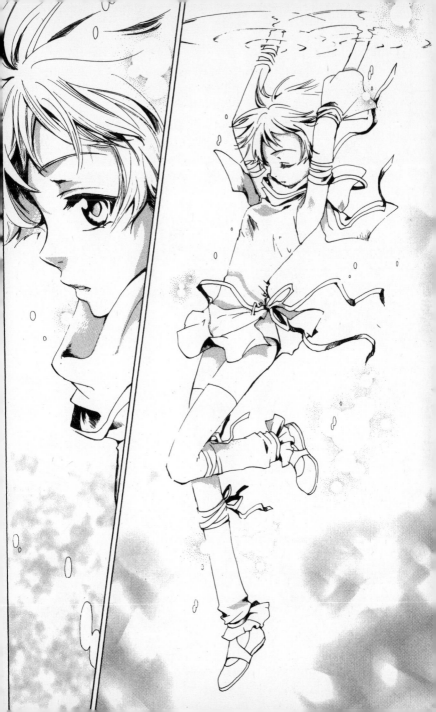

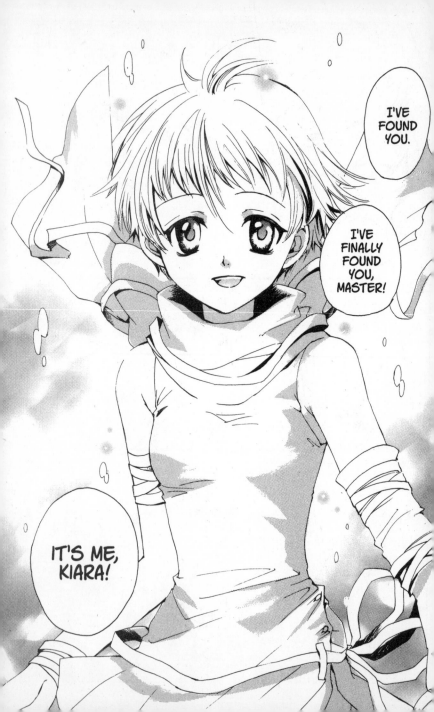

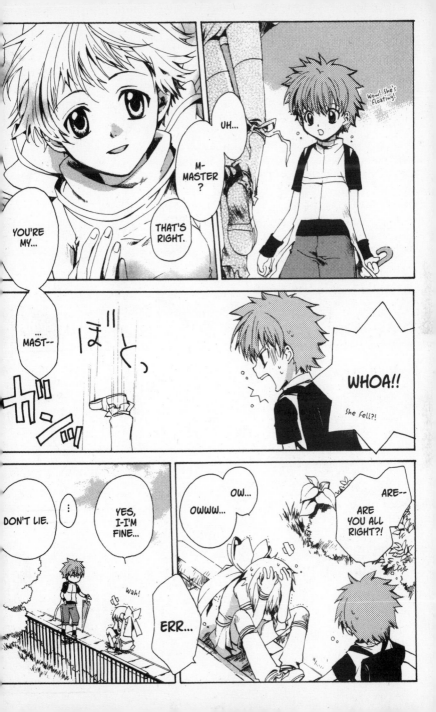

SHE FELL FROM THE SKY.

I WONDER IF SHE'S EVEN HUMAN...

Probably.

SHE MUST BE ABOUT MY SISTER'S AGE.

I'M JUST FINE!

THIS IS ALL PRETTY WEIRD.

SMOOTH SMOOTH

CRAK

CAIK

Eh heh!

Eh heh!

BUT SHE'S PRETTY...

...AND KINDA ENDEARING, SO I GUESS IT'S ALL GOOD.

YES, THEY CALL ME KIARA.

IT'S KIARA, RIGHT?

ARE YOU SOME SORT OF WITCH?

DO YOU COME FROM SOME FANTASY WORLD?

AND WHO'S THIS "MASTER"?

OKAY, NOW I'VE GOT NO CLUE WHAT'S GOING ON.

I DID?

YOU'RE MY MASTER.

NO, NO... I DIDN'T CALL YOU HERE.

I AM HERE ONLY BECAUSE YOU CALLED ME.

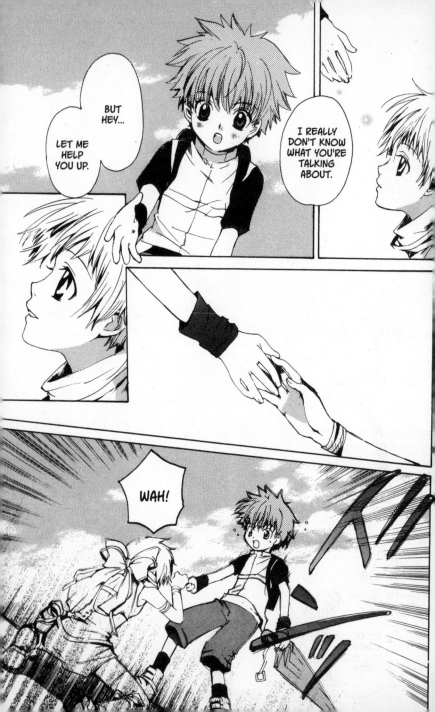

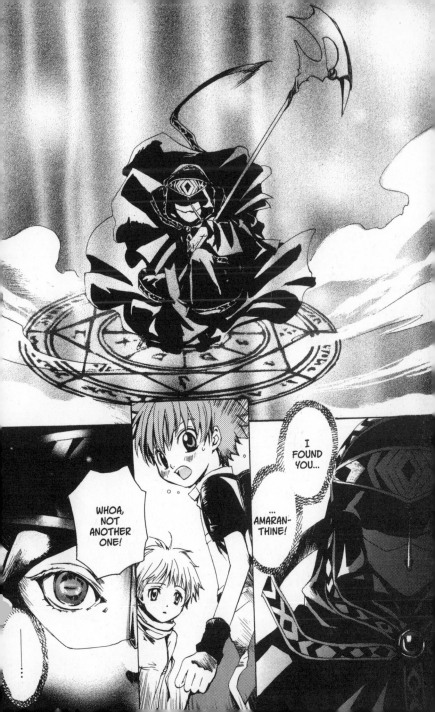

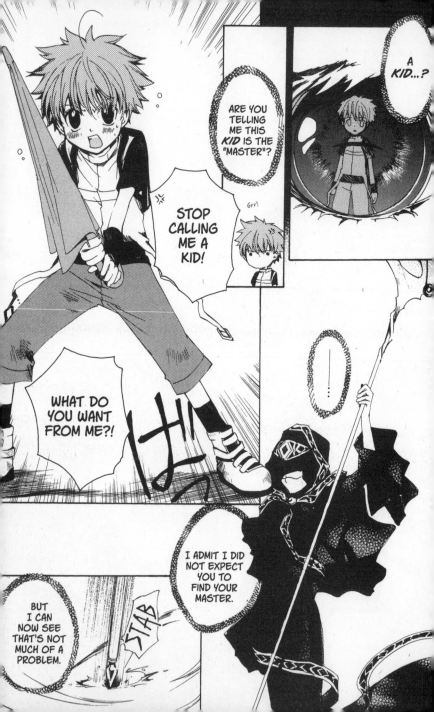

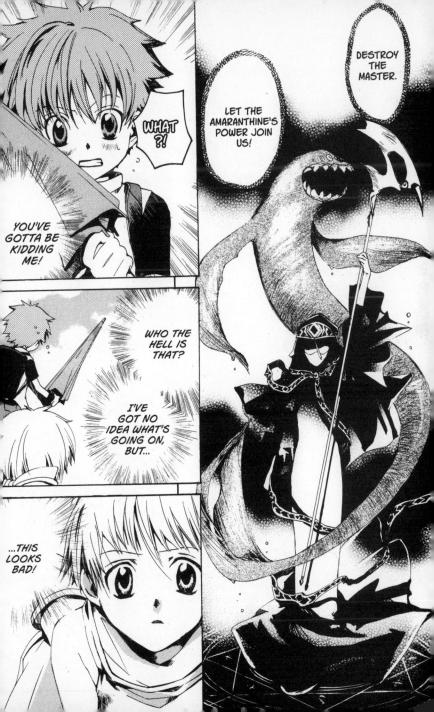

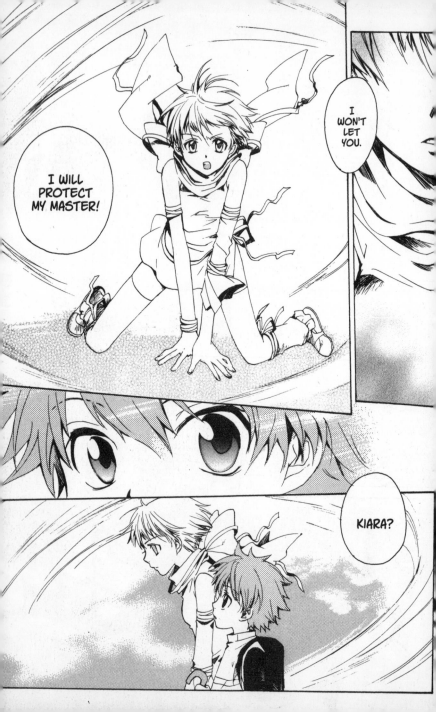

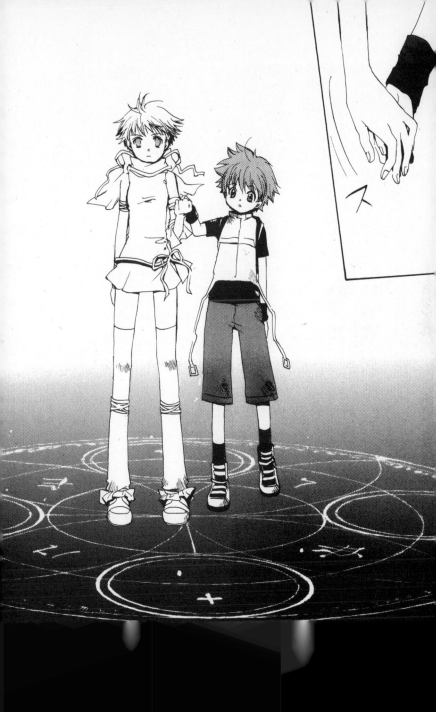

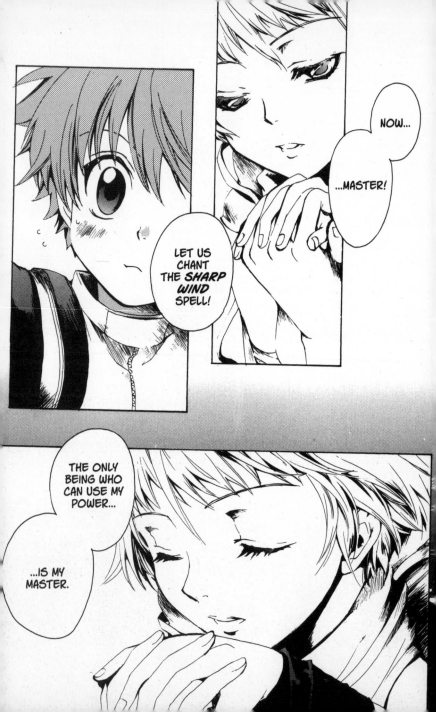

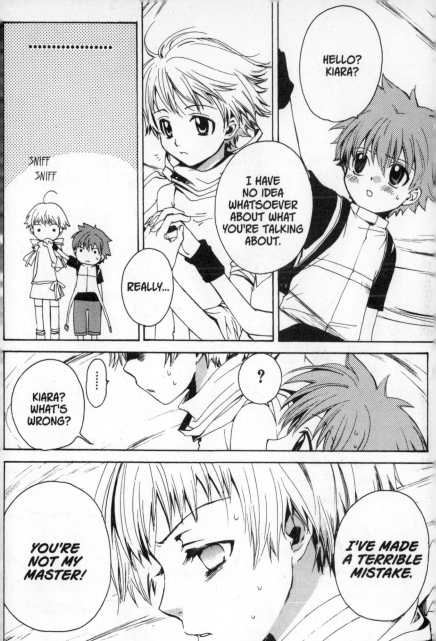

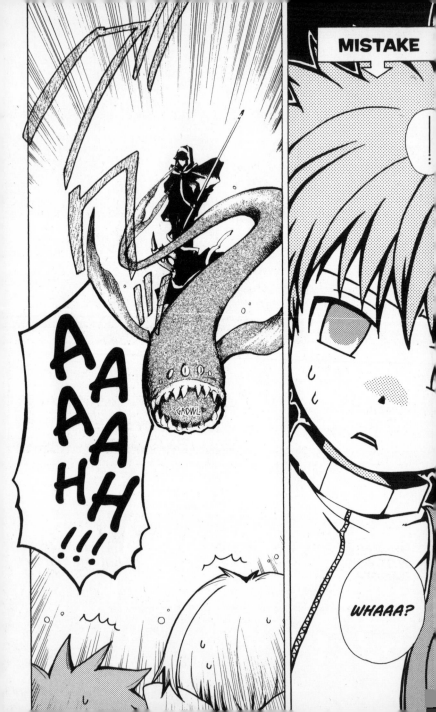

# Don't judge the attorney by her legs.

NINTENDO**DS**.lite   **CAPCOM**

PHOENIX WRIGHT is back, with more challenging cases than ever. Are you a
match for brilliant Franziska von Karma to save your innocent clients from
a lifetime behind bars? Use the microphone and touch screen control
to experience this unbelievably exciting courtroom drama.

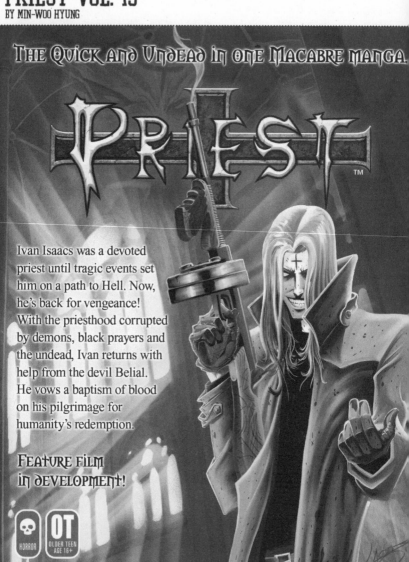

# BLOOD SUCKER™
## ᴗ legend of zipangu ᴗ

**...e Story:**

...ree centuries ago, a vampire named Migiri was running a reign
...terror across Japan, when a hero named Naonosuke cut off his
...ead and sent him to eternal rest...until now. With the help of his
...ght hand man Kuraha, Migiri has been brought back to life and
...anted a sacrifice in the form of the beautiful young Kikuri. The
...ly thing standing in the way of Migiri's restoration is Yusuke
...mukai, who is sworn to protect Kikuri!

**...e Creator:**

...ki Shimizu & Saki Okuse

**...RP:**

...6.99

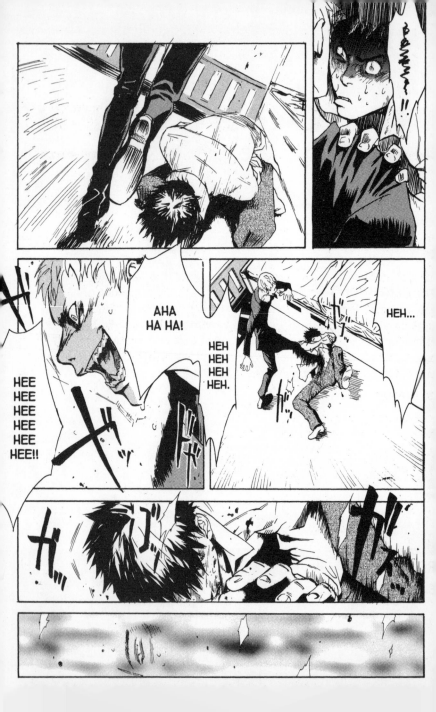

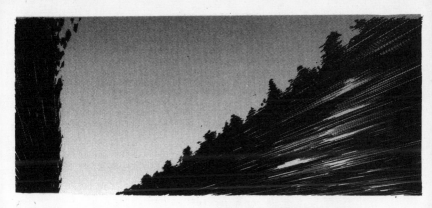

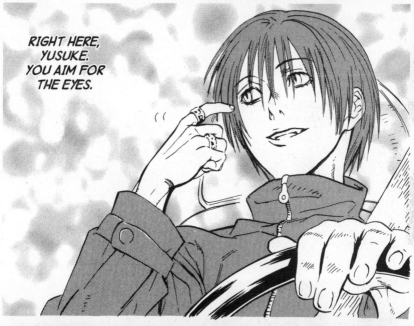

RIGHT HERE,
YUSUKE.
YOU AIM FOR
THE EYES.

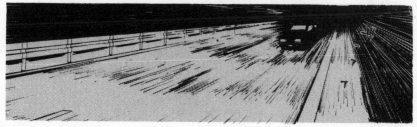

TAKE OUT THE EYES, AND THEY'LL BE OUT OF ACTION FOR A WHILE, THINKING, "OH CRAP! I CAN'T SEE!"

...AT LEAST, TECHNICALLY. BUT IT'S HARD TO GET OVER THE SENSES WE POSSESSED AS HUMANS.

WE CAN UNDERSTAND OUR SURROUND-INGS WITHOUT THE USE OF OUR EYES.

OF COURSE, WHEN YOU REACH KURAHA'S LEVEL, THAT WILL ONLY LAST FOR AN INSTANT.

WHAT CAN I DO, THEN? HOW DO WE KILL THEM?

IF YOU PIERCE THE HEART WITH A CYLINDRICAL OBJECT, NO MATTER WHAT THE MATERIAL IS, THEY'LL TURN TO ASH.

HOWEVER, THE "TURNING INTO ASH" IS REALLY AN ILLUSION. AFTERWARDS YOU WON'T ACTUALLY FIND ANY ASH REMAINING.

THEY SIMPLY CEASE TO BE. YOU'LL FIND YOURSELF FORGETTING ABOUT THEM, LIKE A BAD DREAM.

GUNS WON'T WORK. WHAT'S IMPORTANT IS TO USE AN OBJECT TO CONNECT THE INSIDE AND OUTSIDE. HOW'S THAT FOR PHILOSOPHICAL?

CAN I REALLY
TRUST YOU
RIGHT NOW,
HIKAGE?

YOU JUST AIM
FOR THE EYES.
LEAVE THE REST
TO ME.

31

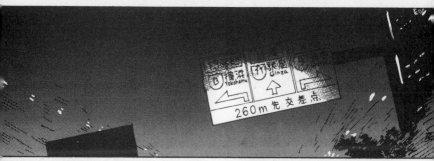

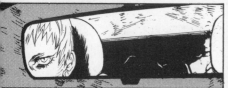

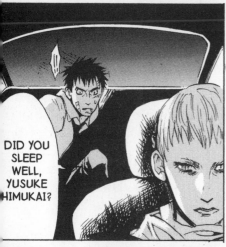

DID YOU
SLEEP
WELL,
YUSUKE
HIMUKAI?

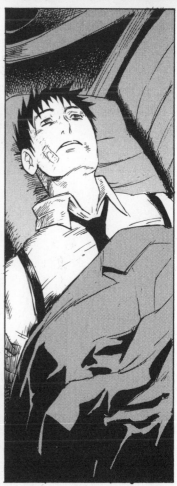

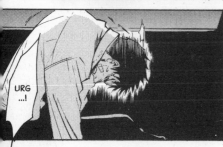

URG
...!

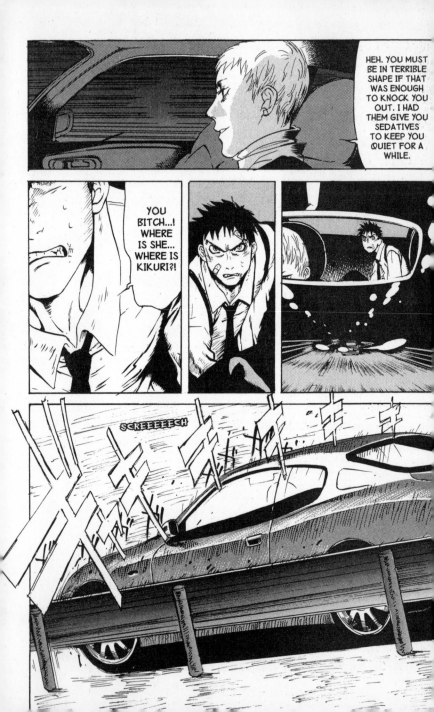

ARE YOU ONE OF THOSE MONSTERS, TOO?! GIVE KIKURI BACK!!

AAGH!!

AAAAAHHH!!

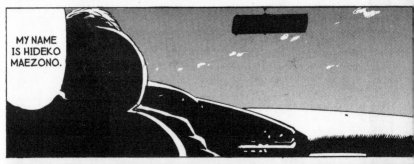

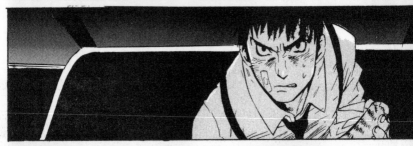

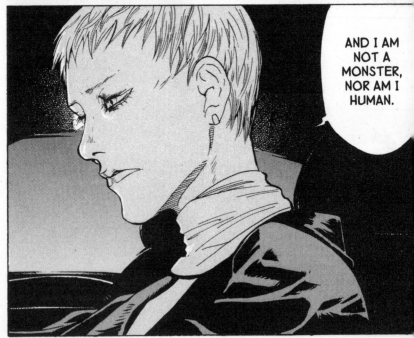

Sign: Checkpoint Ahead

AND WHERE ARE YOU GOING?

JUST FOR A DRIVE.

GOOD EVENING, MA'AM.

IT'S DANGEROUS BEING OUT AT NIGHT. TRY TO AVOID DOING THIS IN THE FUTURE.

TAKE CARE OUT THERE, OFFICER.

IS IT THOSE MAGO-RAKA PEOPLE? IT MUST BE HARD BEING A POLICE-MAN.

PAUSE

GAME GUY

I'VE FOUND HIDEKO MAEZONO FROM THE PUBLIC SAFETY BRANCH. SHE'S ESCORTING A YOUNG MAN.

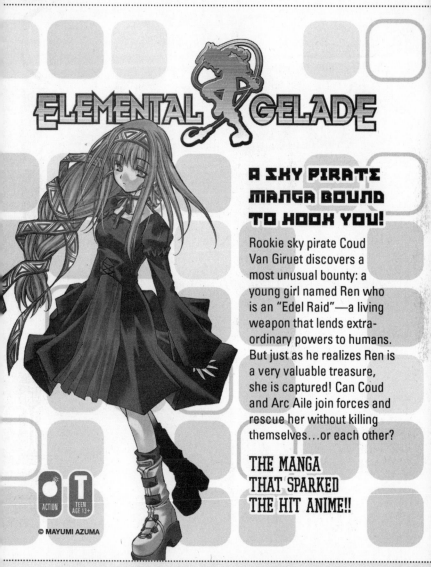

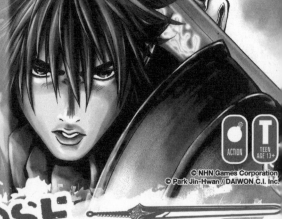

# BUS GAMER™

## 1999→2001 THE PILOT EDITION

### The Story:

Toki Mishiba, Nobuto Nakajyo, and Kazuo Saitoh are hired to play the Biz Game, a game much like capture the flag, only with company secrets and insane amounts of money involved. At first they think it's a crazy but fun way to get some money, but as the game goes on, they hear stories about mysterious deaths on the news, and recognize the victims as members of the teams they've beaten in the game. When one of the losers of a game dies right in front of them, they realize what is really at stake--their very lives!

### The Creator:

Kazuya Minekura

ACTION

OT
OLDER TEEN
AGE 16+

### SRP:

£6.99

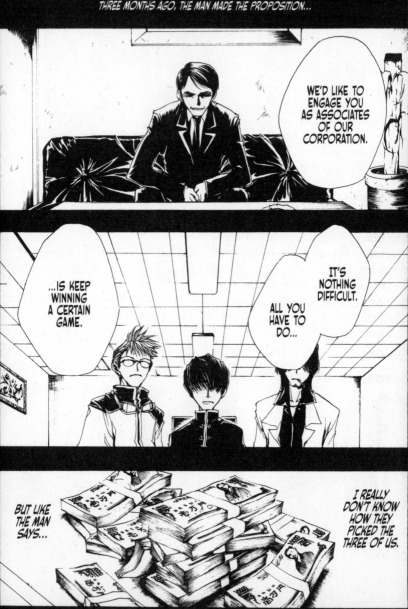

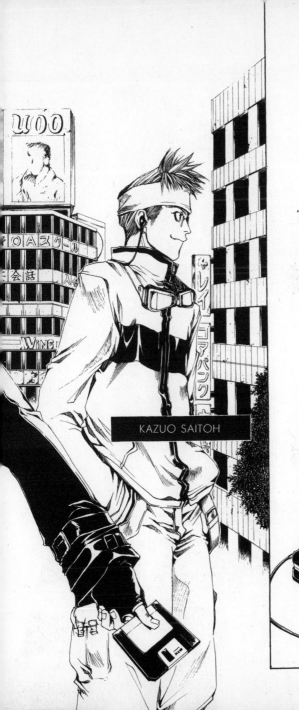

...MONEY IS MONEY.

KAZUO SAITOH

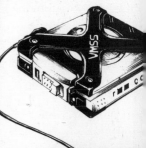

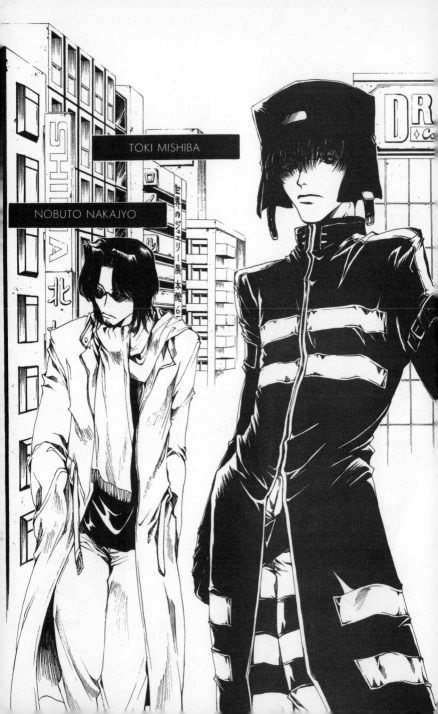

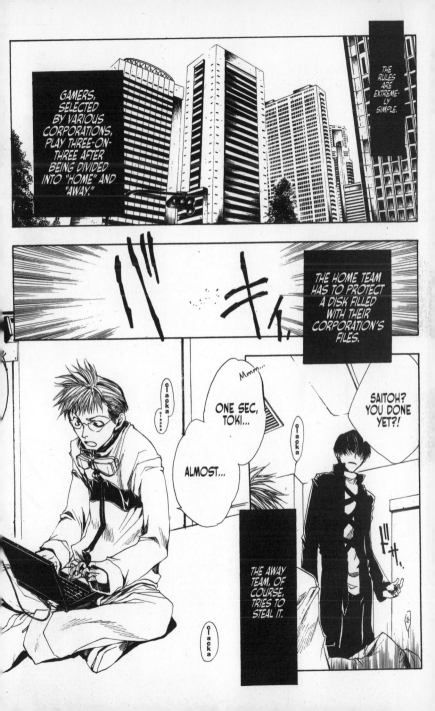

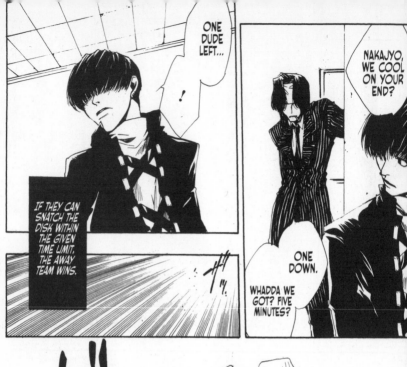

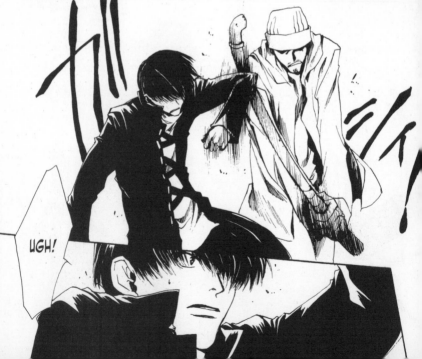

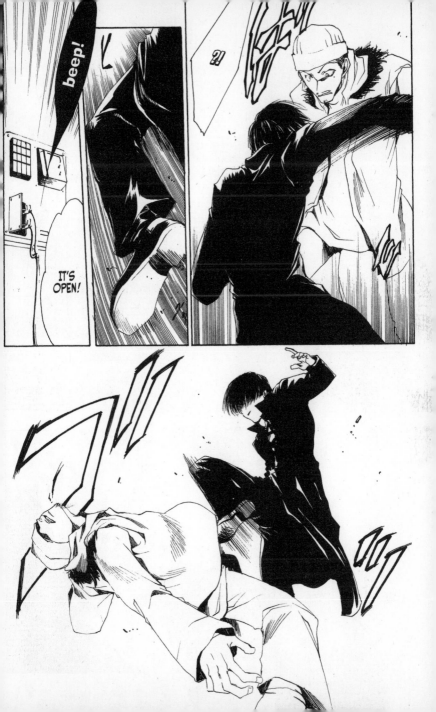

GAME OVER!!

YEAH, BABY.

IT'S A STUPID GAME. THIS IS HOW CRAZY RICH PEOPLE AMUSE THEMSELVES.

AND WE'RE THEIR PAWNS.

# STAGE 1 : The Curtain Rises

Hn....

THEY'D BETTER BE.

THIS MAKES EIGHT WINS IN A ROW.

YOUR RECRUITS ARE EXCELLENT, MR. KAICHOU.

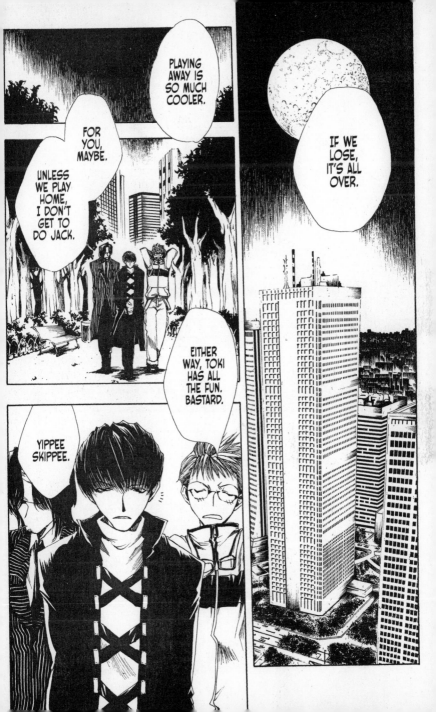

TEAM AAA? TRIPLE ANONYMOUS, RIGHT?

SO, EIGHT IN A ROW, EH?

IF THAT'S WHAT YOU CALL YOURSELVES, YOU OBVIOUSLY DON'T GIVE A SHIT.

WHO THE HELL ARE YOU?

OH...LIKE US...

I'M A BUSINESS GAMER.

I'M NOT JACKING OFF FOR JOLLIES.

NO. NOT LIKE YOU AT ALL.

......

HMM...

JOLLIES...?

LOOK, DUDE, IT'S JUST A GAME, RIGHT?

50

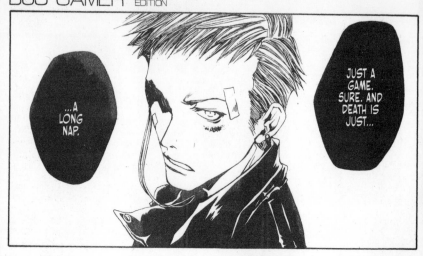

...A LONG NAP.

JUST A GAME. SURE. AND DEATH IS JUST...

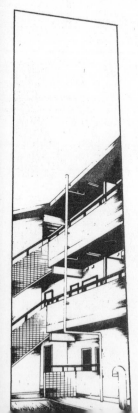

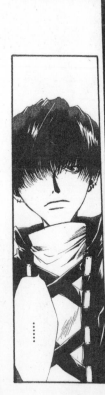

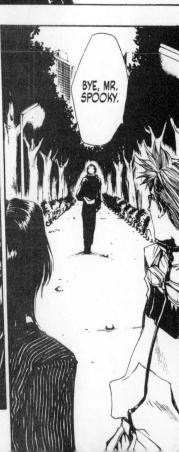

BYE, MR. SPOOKY.

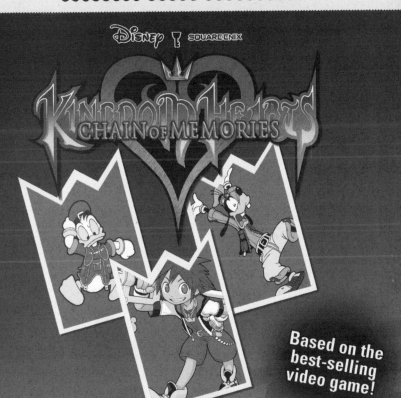

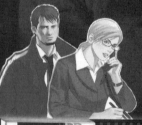

# DAZZLE ™

## The Story:

When 14-year-old Rahzel's father suddenly kicked her out of the house to go on a training journey and hone her magical abilities, he didn't expect her to immediately fall in with Alzeid, an albino magic user in search of his father's killer. Alzeid is a loner with little sense of humor, but when Rahzel swears to take his stupid, boring life and change it into something worth smiling about, he dares her to try. Though their companionship is rocky at first, after a few magical misadventures, their relationship is starting to bud.

Now, a few weeks into their journey, Rahzel gets sidetracked when she sees a little boy named Vincent being picked on by some thugs. When she beats up his attackers, she earns his undying gratitude, but his guardians Baroqueheat and Soresta are not so amused when they catch up to him. Rahzel rises to Vincent's defense once again when Soresta starts punishing him for running off, and this sets in motion a chain of events that will change their lives forever...

## The Creator:

Minari Endoh

DRAMA

OT
OLDER TEEN
AGE 16+

## SRP:

£6.99

### Sea Horse
**(Syngnathidae)**

[known as *umasao* or *tatsu no otoshigo* in Japan] It's a small fish with a thin layer of skin stretched over a series of bony plates, with bony bumps visible as rings around the trunk. It eats plankton or other small fish.

**Brood Pouch**

YOU SHOULD COME BACK AFTER BEING APPRENTICED TO A SEA HORSE...

...YOU BEAU-TIFUL BIG BROTHER, YOU.

SUCH A SWEET THING FOR THE GIRL TO SAY, NO?

Male sea horses raise the children. What role models, huh?

IT'S THE GUARDIAN'S FAULT IF THE CHILD GETS LOST!

Ah ha ha!

**YOU** SURE SEEM TO BE **ENJOYING THIS!**

**YOU'RE LOWER THAN SEAFOOD, SORESTA!**

THEN AT LEAST TRY NOT TO LAUGH AT ME!

FIRST OF ALL, **YOU** ARE THE ONE WHO WAS INSULTED, NOT **ME.**

Plus, I really don't care.

AS A GENTLEMAN, I **SHUN** VIOLENCE.

AREN'T YOU MAD THAT SHE **INSULTED US?** DO SOMETHING ABOUT IT!

...UNLIKE HIM, I AM **NOT** GENEROUS ENOUGH TO LAUGH AND FORGIVE YOU...

...AFTER BEING HUMILIATED SO!

ALL RIGHT. ALL RIGHT...

Bwaaah ha ha!

ANYWAY...

Wah ha ha!

BUT I JUST CAN'T HELP IT!

HOWEVER...

SO I'M GOING TO SLICE YOUR *PRETTY* FACE TO *RIBBONS!*

...YOU'RE *NOT MY TYPE!*

WOW! THANKS FOR SAYING I'M PRETTY!

YOU'RE PRETTY HANDSOME YOURSELF!

...IDIOT!!

YOU...

ALZEID?!

SORESTA, BAROQUE-HEAT...

I'M SORRY THAT MY FRIEND CAUSED YOU TROUBLE.

Why am I the bad guy here?!

Hey!?

LONG TIME NO SEE.

EHH?! YOU KNOW THEM?!

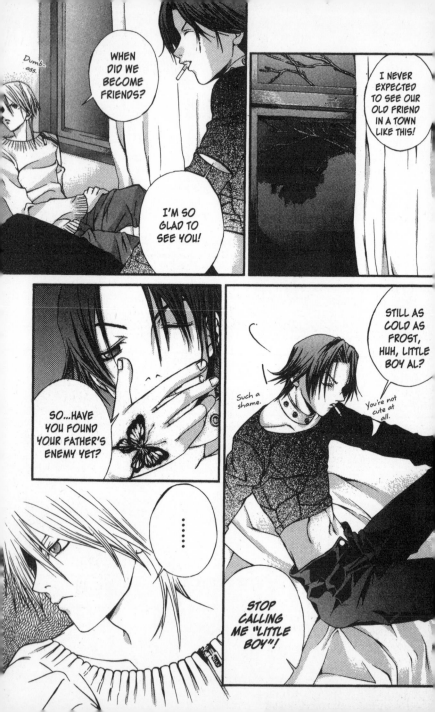

BUT FOR NOW, LET'S JUST BE HAPPY...

...THAT WE'VE FINALLY BEEN REUNITED!

Did you wash off the garbage smell yet?

Shut up!

YOU WILL EVENTUALLY.

BY THE WAY... WHO'S THE GIRL?

YOU MEAN RAHZEL?

YOU'RE A DEAD MAN.

SORRY!

NOW I SEE WHY YOU NEVER HAD ANY GIRLFRIENDS BEFORE!

RAHZEL, IS IT?

I HAD NO IDEA YOU HAD A LOLITA COMPLEX!

SHE AND I DON'T HAVE THAT KIND OF RELATION-SHIP.

SO DON'T WASTE YOUR TIME.

SHE PACKS A LOT INTO THAT SMALL PACKAGE!

ENOUGH WITH THE SICK OLD MAN PORN JOKES.

DON'T GET ME WRONG...I *LOVE* SEX--BUT *HATE* KIDS.

YOU KIDDING ME?

I'm just imagining her future self!

That girl is an exception.

WHEN DID YOU BE-COME A DAD, BAROQUE-HEAT?

BESIDES THAT... WHO'S THE KID?

YOU WANNA JOIN US? THE MONEY'S GOOD.

NO THANKS...

IT'S OUR JOB TO TAKE HIM BACK TO HIS PARENTS.

HE'S AN IL-LEGITIMATE CHILD.

VINCENT IS A RICH KID.

I bought things for us!

HOW *DARE* YOU ATTACK ME LIKE THAT WHEN *YOU'RE* THE ONE WHO SENT ME OUT SHOPPING?!

THOSE SURE ARE A LOT OF BAGS.

DON'T TELL ME YOU BOUGHT CLOTHES AGAIN.

I'M BACK!

I KNEW THEM WHEN I WAS IN THE ARMY.

Hello.

Hi.

I NEVER INTRODUCED YOU TO THEM. THIS IS SORESTA AND BAROQUEHEAT.

SHE IS...

...MY PARTNER.

THE ARMY?!

HUH?!

NICE TO MEET YOU...

Can we eat now?

THIS LITTLE ONE IS RAHZEL.

What?!

*YOU* USED TO BE IN THE *ARMY?!*

YEAH, BEFORE.

WELL, I CAN CERTAINLY SEE THE POTENTIAL HERE.

Grr...

SHE'LL BE ONE HOT BABE IN THE NEAR FUTURE.

PARTNER?

I SEE...

What of it?!

YEAH, I AM!

So cute.

YOU A VIRGIN?

AND *YOU* STOP RISING TO HIS BAIT.

STOP BAITING HER.

HUH?

DON'T COME NEAR ME! YOU STINK LIKE CIGA-RETTES!

He wants something in his mouth.

......

Where's an ash-tray?

AL, AL... LITTLE BOY...

IF YOU'RE NOT INTERESTED IN TOUCHING HER, THEN WHY NOT GIVE HER TO ME?

*I told you not to call me "little boy"!*

DON'T ASK *ME.*

THEN I'LL ASK *HER!*

HEY, RAHZEL... WANNA BE MY GIRL?

NO WAY!

OON'T BE SO RIENDLY, ERVERT!

YOU SEE, FLOWERS HAVE A STAMEN AND A PISTIL...

I DON'T THINK YOU'RE HELPING...

WHAT'S A VIRGIN?

ALZEID! THIS BASTARD IS YOUR *FRIEND,* ISN'T HE?! *DO SOMETHING!!*

OON'T OW YOU! EFUSE TO EMEMBER OUR NAME! ALREADY RGOT YOU!

DON'T CALL ME "BASTARD" LIKE YOU DON'T LIKE ME!

CALL ME BAROQUE-HEAT!

*Let me go!*

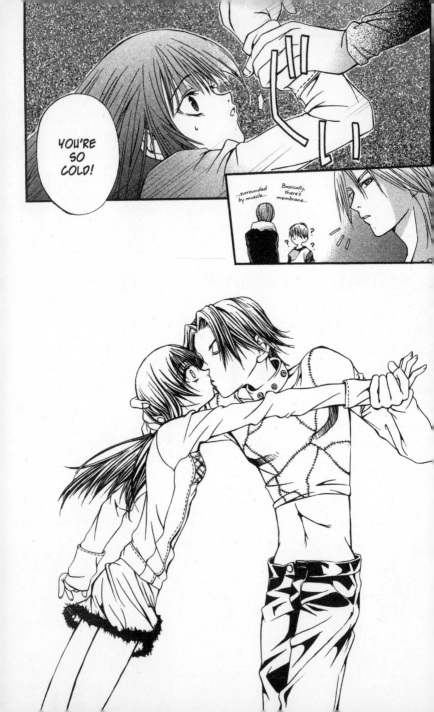

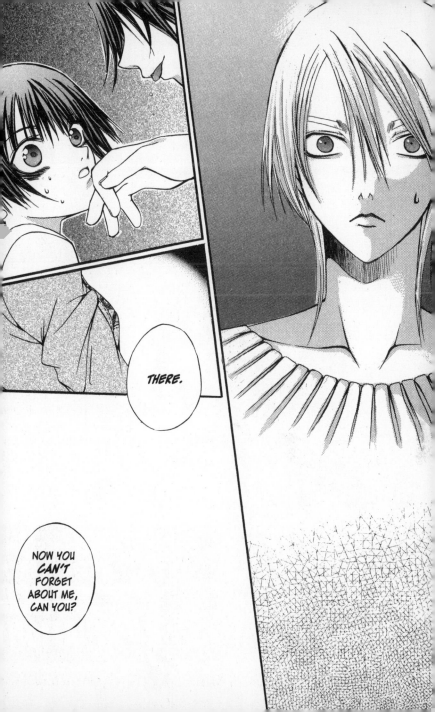

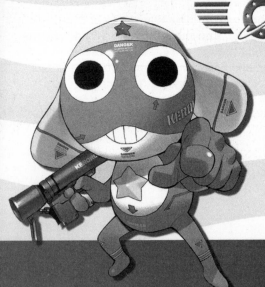

# THE GOOD WITCH OF THE WEST™

**he Story:**

Fifteen year old Firiel lives in the remote highlands with her
father, a recluse obsessed with astronomy. Yet, life is more than
pleasant for Firiel--her father's servants adore her, his kindly
apprentice Rune is her best friend, and she's about to attend the
count's ball! But as Firiel prepares for the gala, she discovers her
past is more complicated than she had thought--and she may be the
heir to the throne! Unaware of the danger that faces her and all
she loves, Firiel begins a courageous quest for the truth.

**he Creator:**

Haruhiko Momokawa & Noriko Ogiwara

FANTASY

T

TEEN
AGE 13+

**RP:**

6.99

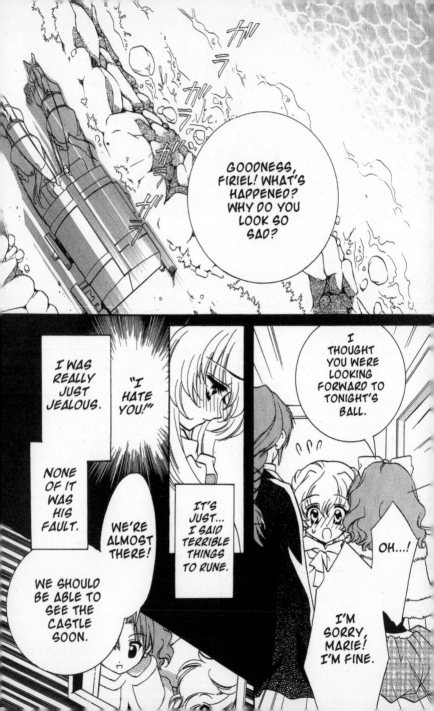

THERE IT IS! FLYING SWALLOW CASTLE--THE COUNT OF RUALGO'S ESTATE HERE AT AMBERPOINTE.

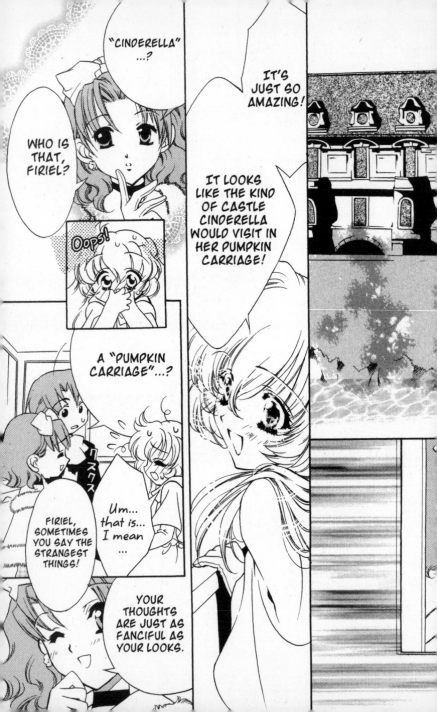

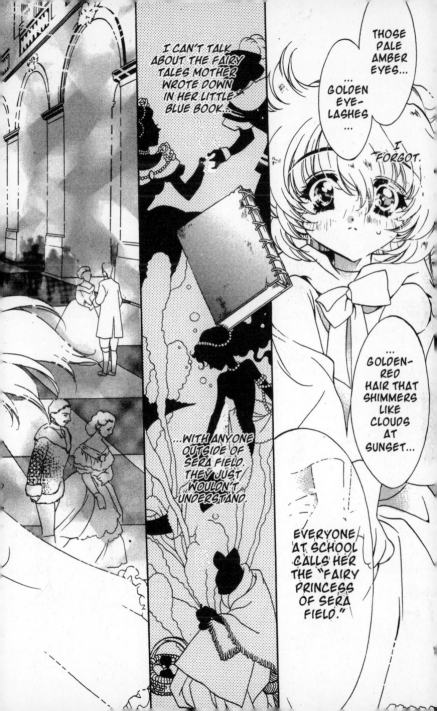

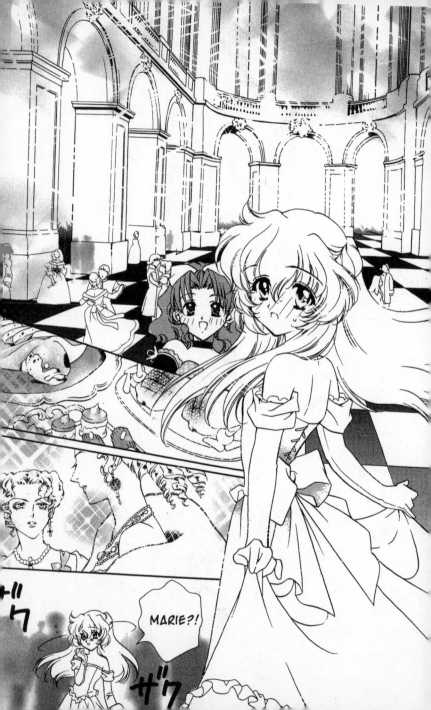

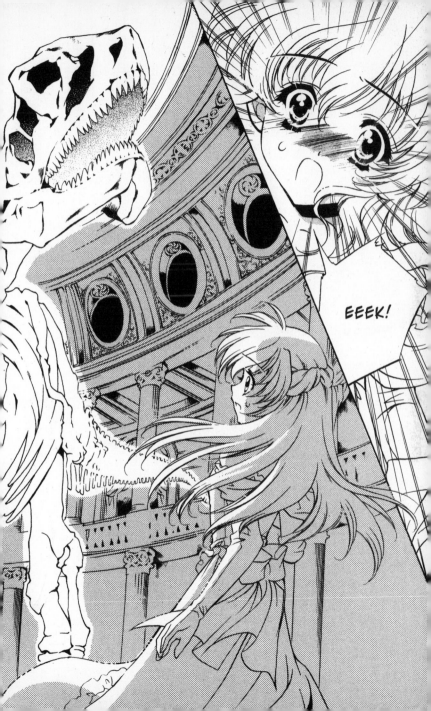

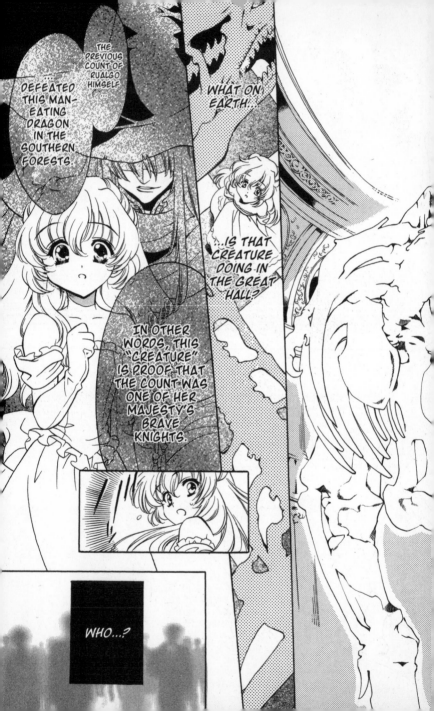

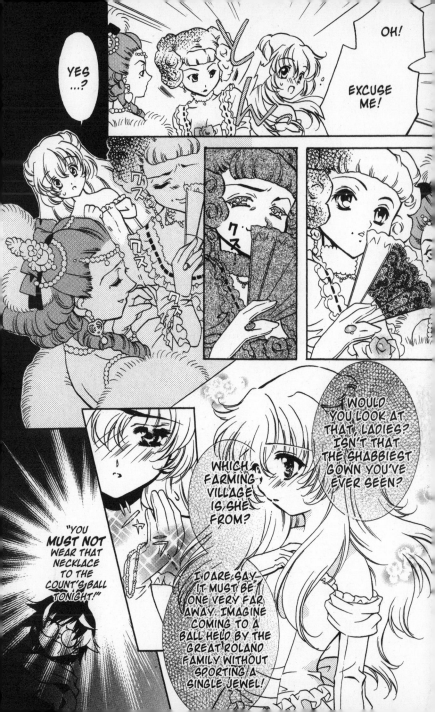

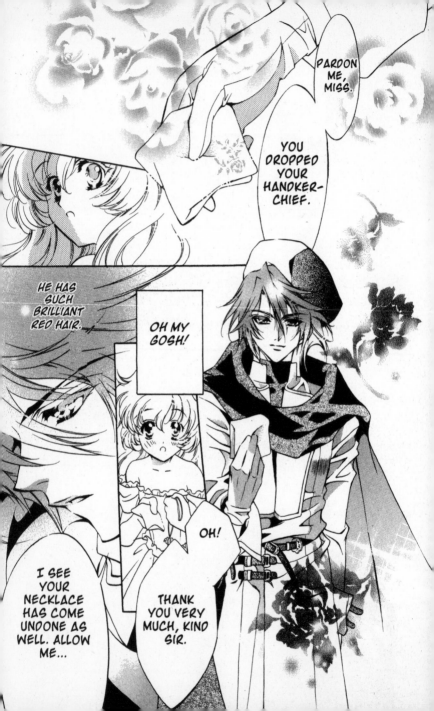

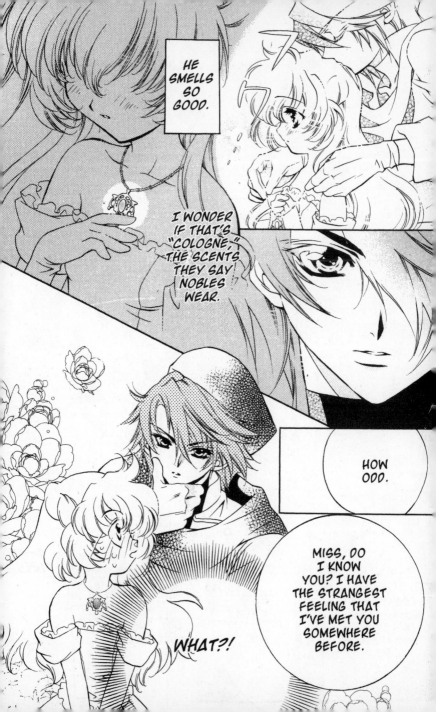

I-I'M CALLED FIRIEL DEE, MY LORD.

WOULD YOU BE SO KIND AS TO TELL ME YOUR NAME?

I'M FROM SERA FIELD...

HE'S THE HEIR TO THE COUNTY OF RUALGO?!

I AM EUGIS ROLAND...

...AND I SWEAR I HAVE NEVER SEEN YOU BEFORE TODAY!

...ELDEST SON OF THE COUNT OF RUALGO.

I CAN'T BELIEVE HE'S ACTUALLY TALKING TO ME!

I DIDN'T KNOW PEOPLE...

SERA FIELD?!

PER-HAPS, MY LORD!

...STILL LIVED IN THOSE HIGHLANDS. THEN PERHAPS I AM MIS-TAKEN.

HE'S JUST LIKE THE PRINCE CHARMING IN MOTHER'S FAIRY TALES.

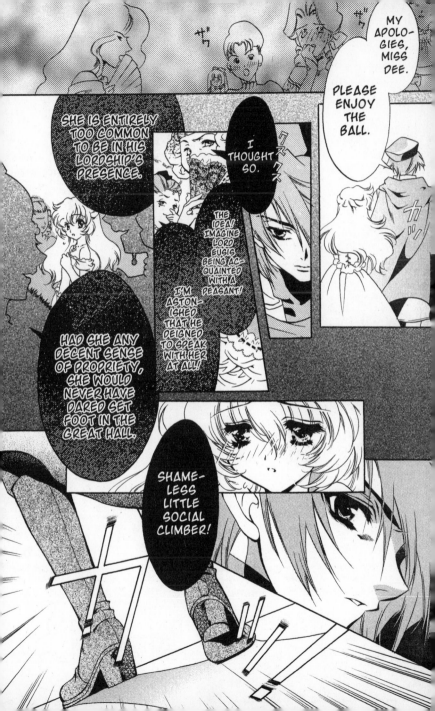

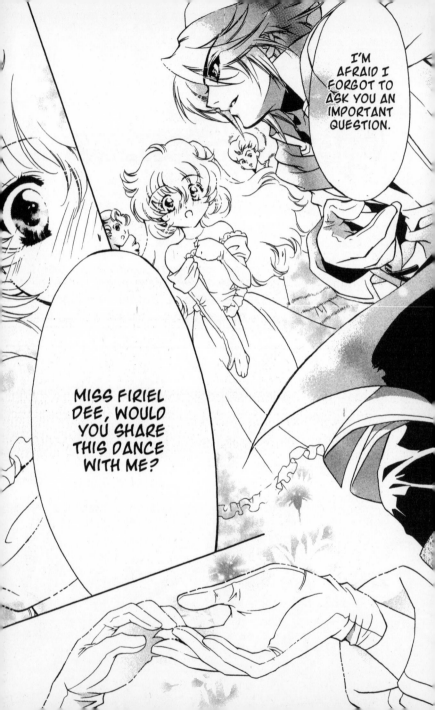

## The Story:

Anya is a young girl in tenth grade who has to adjust to her new school. When she tries to join the various school sports teams she's rejected...so she forms her own soccer team, complete with cool uniforms. And thus begins the first Gothic-Lolita soccer team!

## The Creator:

Anike Hage

DRAMA

T

TEEN
AGE 13+

## SRP:

£6.99

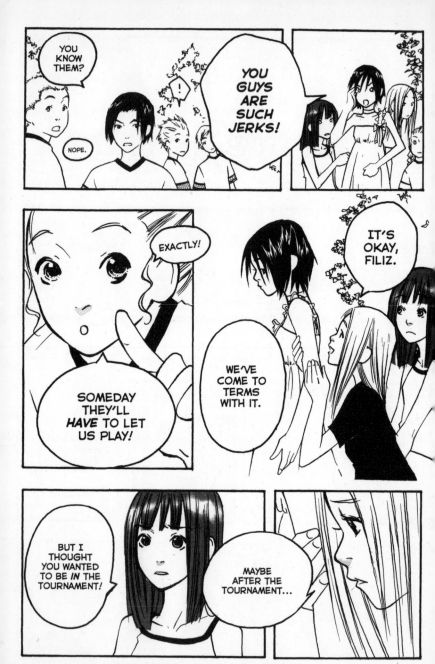

WE SHOULD START OUR OWN TEAM, JUST TO SPITE THEM!

UGH... THAT'S SO UNFAIR!

HMM. IN THEORY...

UH, YEAH. THAT WOULD TOTALLY BREAK THEIR HEARTS.

YOU KNOW WHAT I MEAN!

YOU JUST NEED PERMISSION FROM THE PRINCIPAL.

SURE!

...CAN FEMALE STUDENTS EVEN START THEIR OWN TEAMS?

ARE YOU THINKING WHAT I'M THINKING?

HM?

JULIA...?

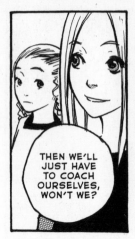

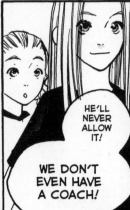

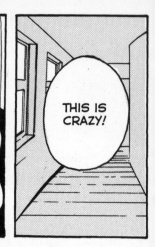

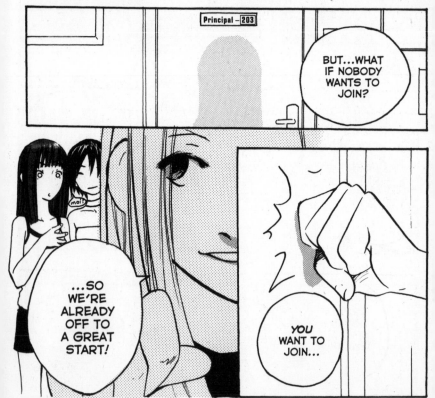

Principal — 203

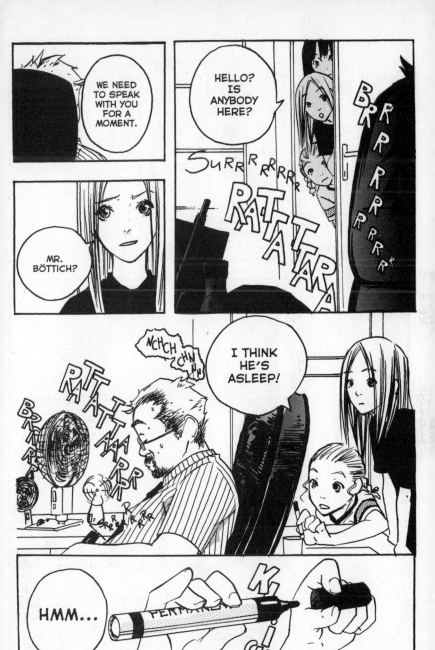

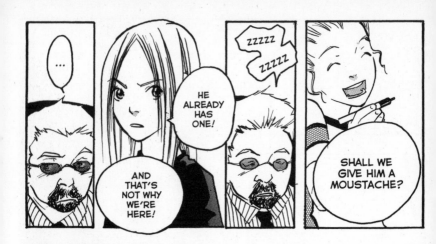

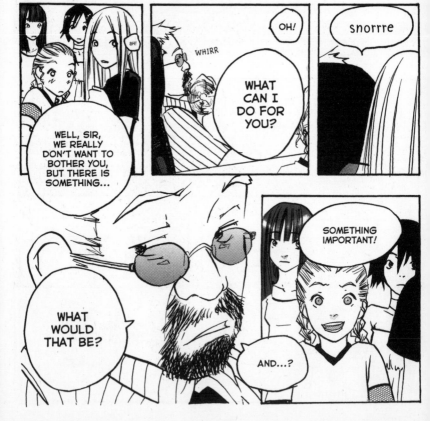

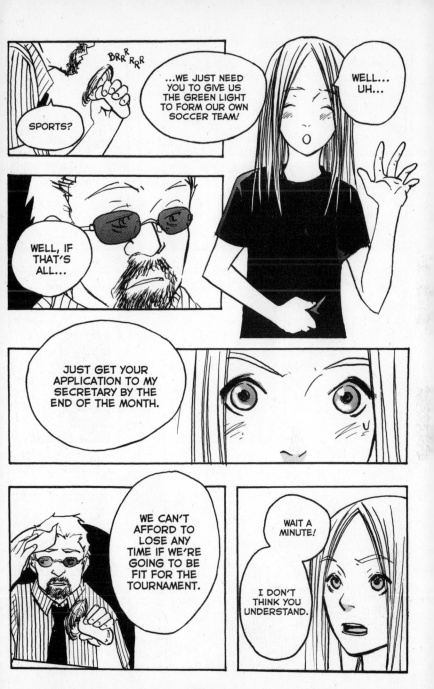

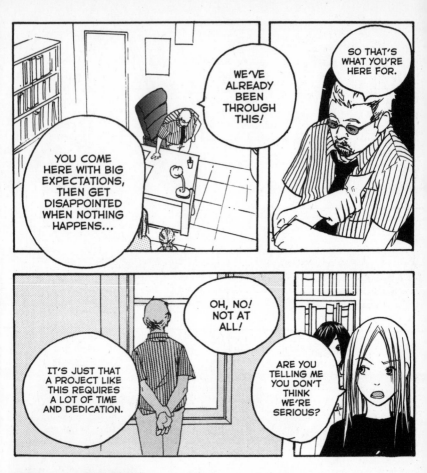

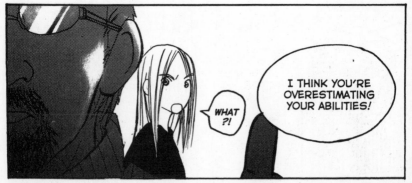

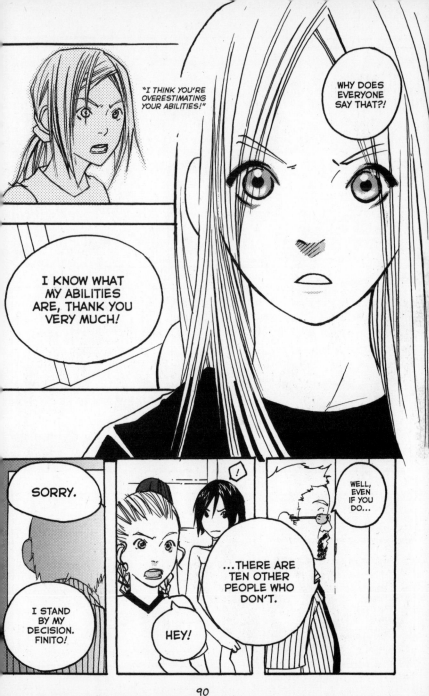

COULD YOU STEP OUTSIDE FOR A MOMENT?

GALS...

HM?

WE NEED TO HAVE A PRIVATE CHAT.

THIS CAN'T BE GOOD.

...

WHAT'S SHE PLANNING?

NO PROBLEM.

WE'LL BE IN THE HALLWAY IF YOU NEED US.

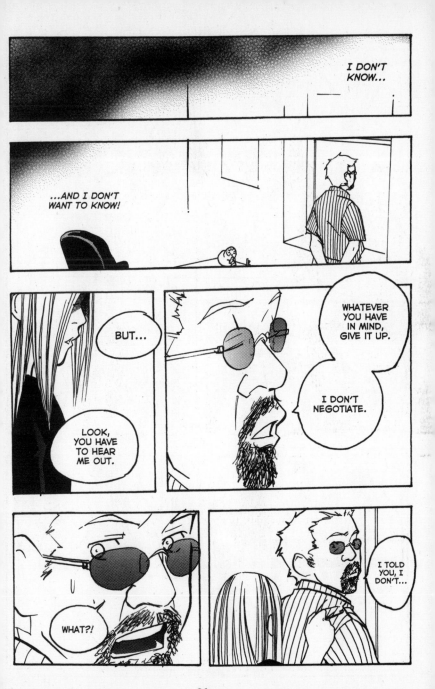

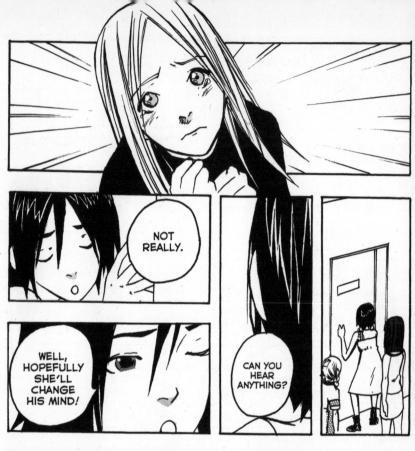

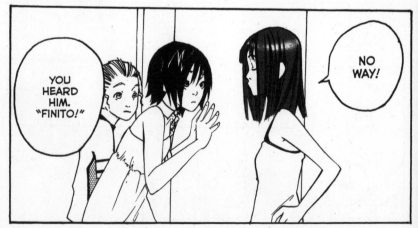

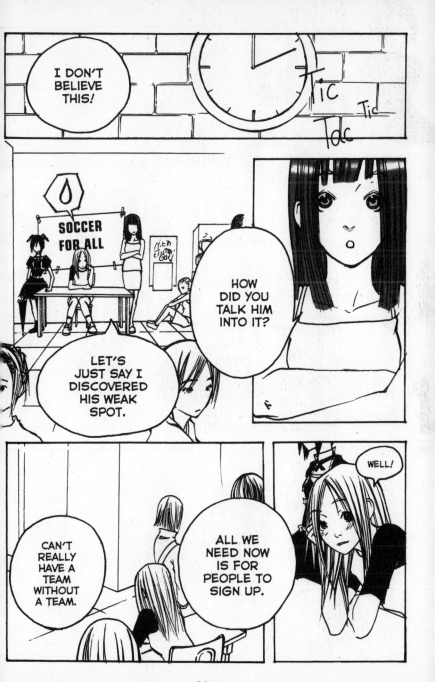

94

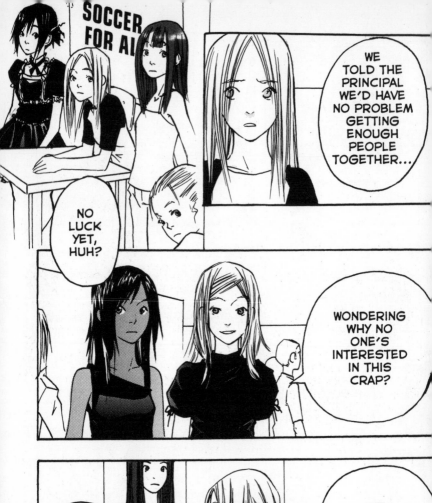
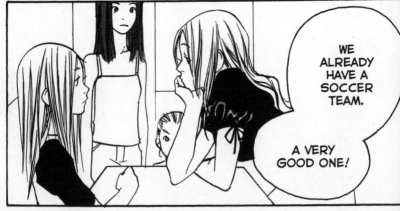

...BUT YOU MUST REALLY ENJOY IT!

YOU KNOW...

MOST PEOPLE DON'T GO IN FOR CONSTANT HUMILIATION...

SEE YOU AROUND!

ANYWAY...

SOCCER FOR ALL

HUNH. THAT ACTUALLY HADN'T OCCURRED TO ME.

JUST LOOK AROUND...

WHAT IF NOBODY DOES WANT TO JOIN OUR TEAM?

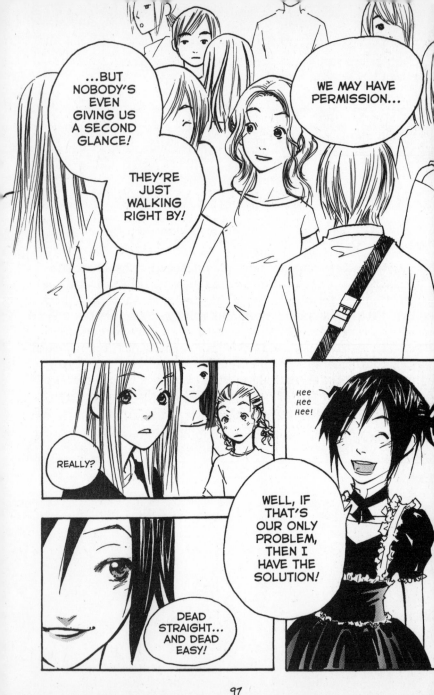

97

# KING of THORN

## The Story:

Twin sisters...Separated by fate...Drawn together by a horrific illness...Kasumi and her sister, Shizuku, were infected with the Medusa virus, which slowly turns the victim to stone--and there is no cure! Hope for salvation rests in Kasumi and a select few who are put into a cryogenically frozen state until a cure is found. But Shizuku is left behind, and in the not-too-distant future, Kasumi awakens to find herself in an unfamiliar world with terrifying beings roaming the terrain. Resolving to unlock the mysteries of the disease and the fate of her twin sister, Kasumi struggles to survive in this treacherous world!

## The Creator:

Yuji Iwahara

ACTION

OT
OLDER TEEN
AGE 16+

## SRP:

£6.99

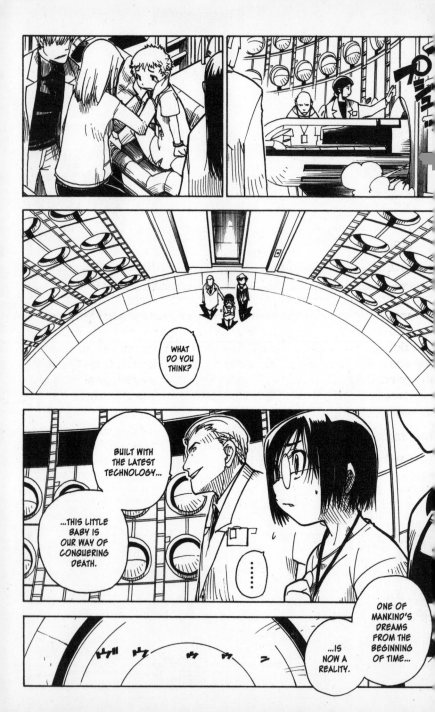

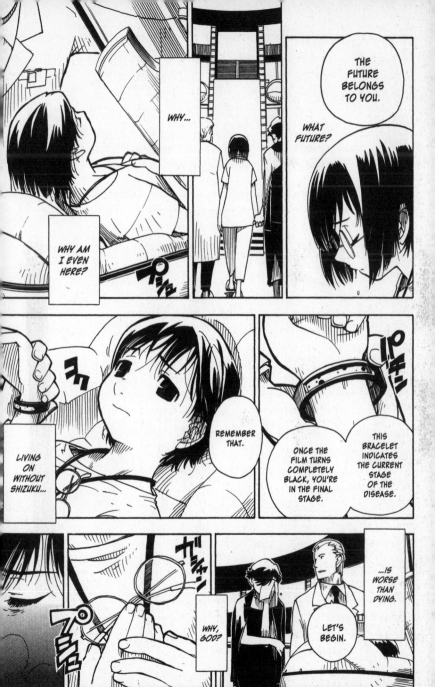

SHYUUUUUU

LIVE...

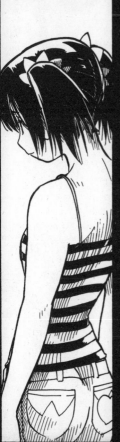

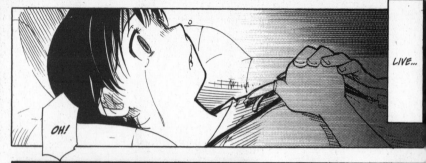

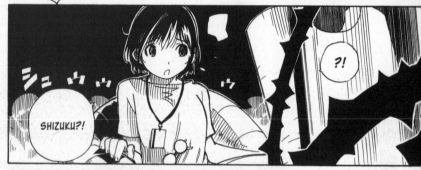

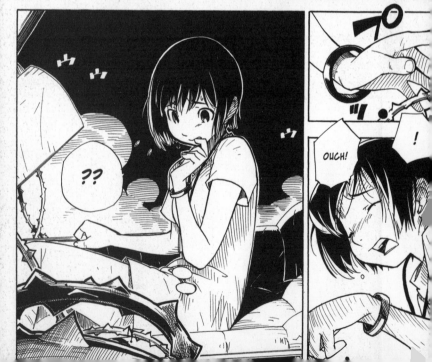

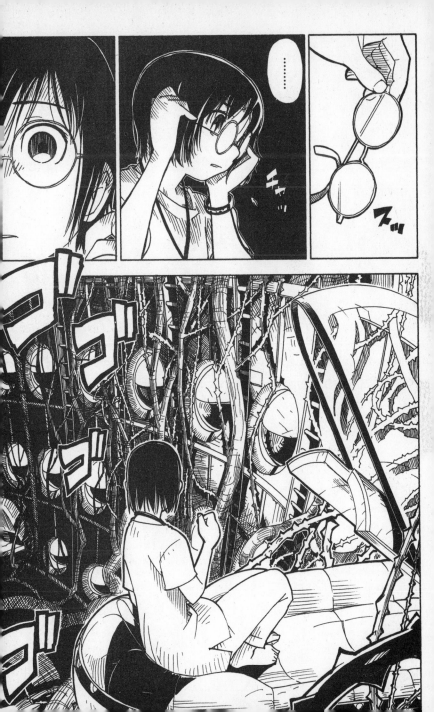

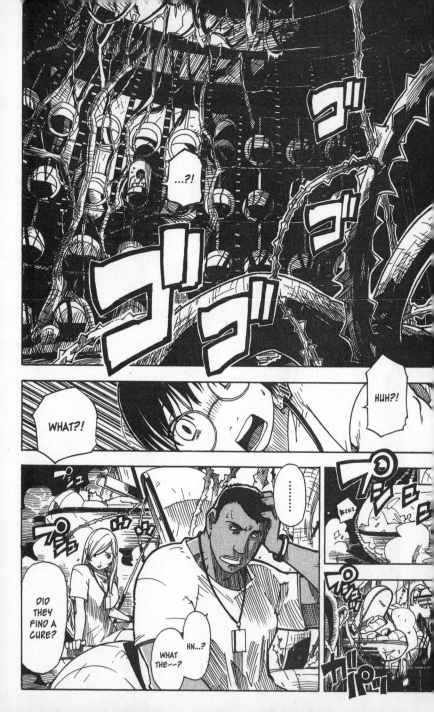

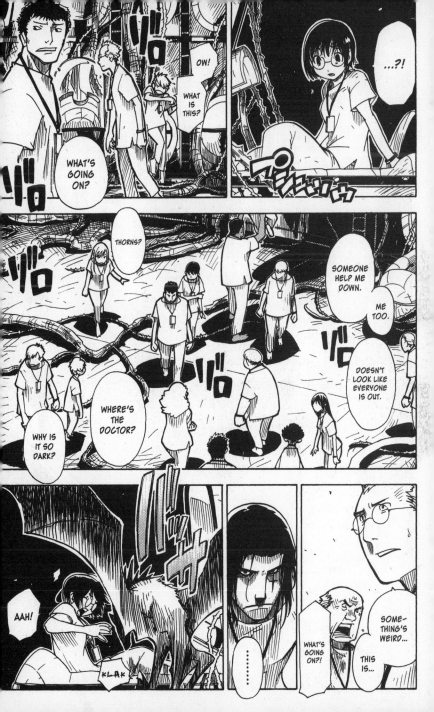

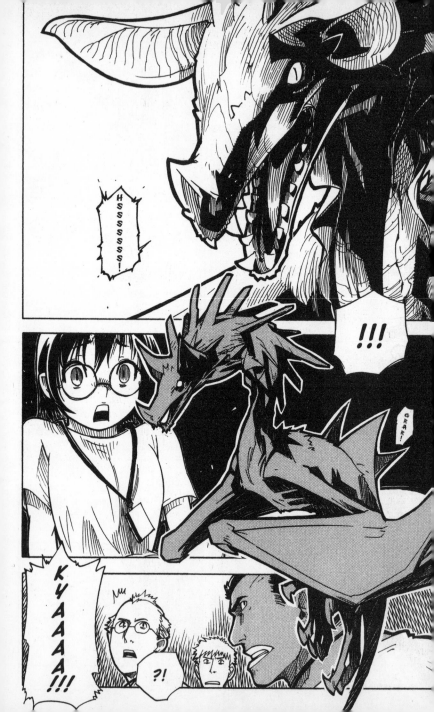

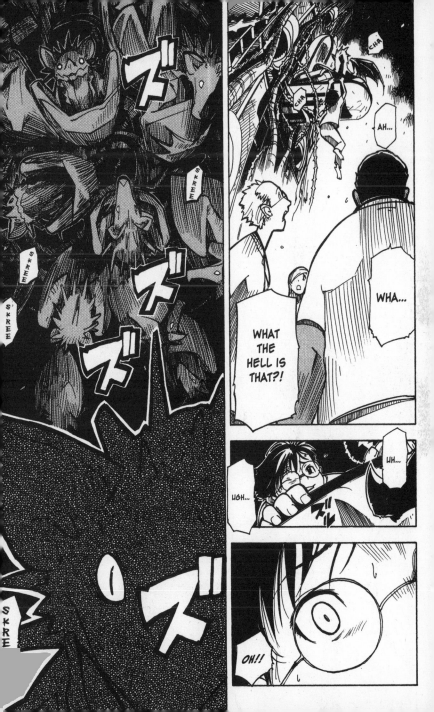

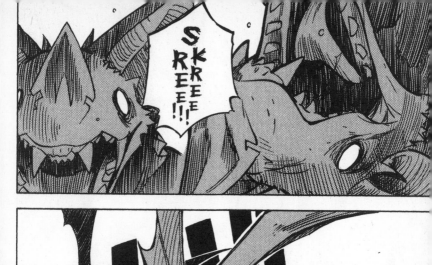

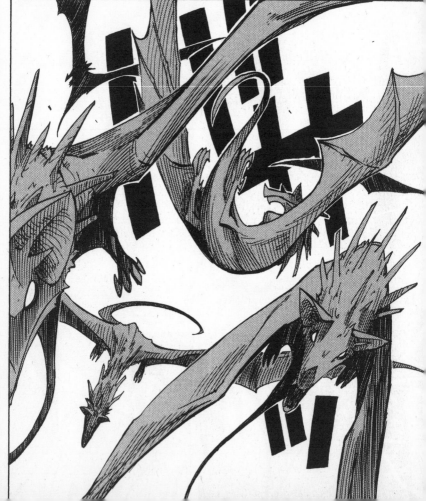

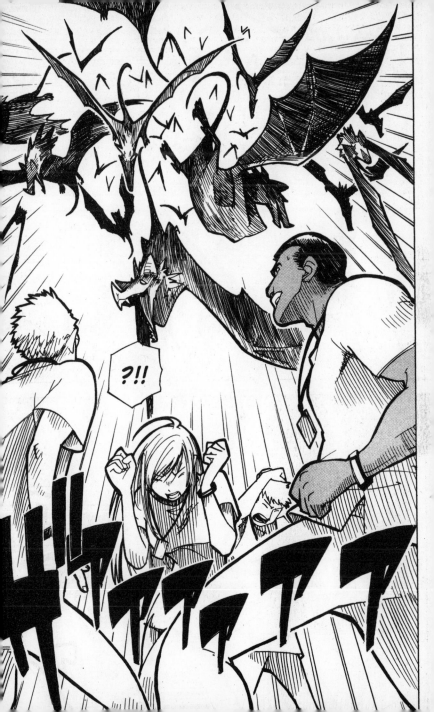

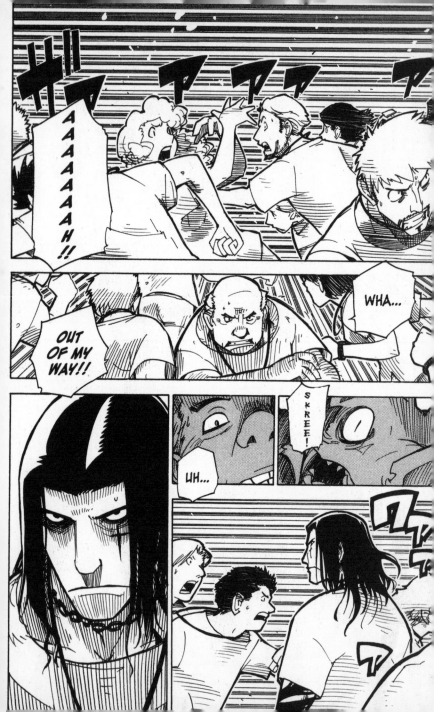

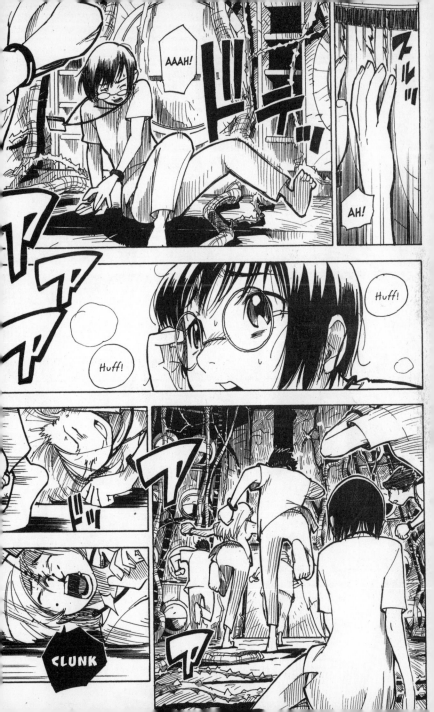

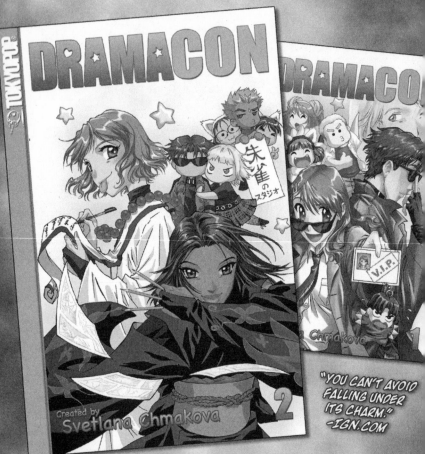

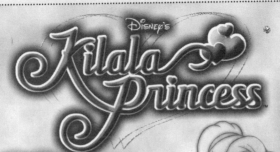
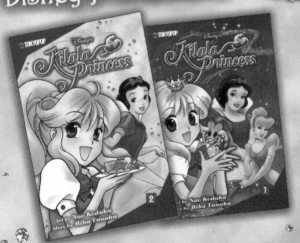

## The Story:

Kantarou, a folklore scholar living in the Taisho period, has various and sundry adventures. But Kantarou moonlights as an exorcist solving the problems of ghosts and demons, all with the help of Haruka, the legendary demon-eating tengu!

## The Creator:

Kazuko Higashiyama & Sakura Kinoshita

COMEDY

T

TEEN
AGE 13+

## SRP:

£6.99

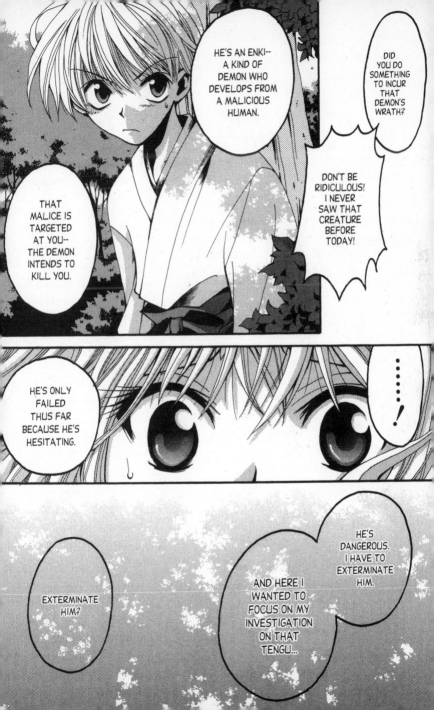

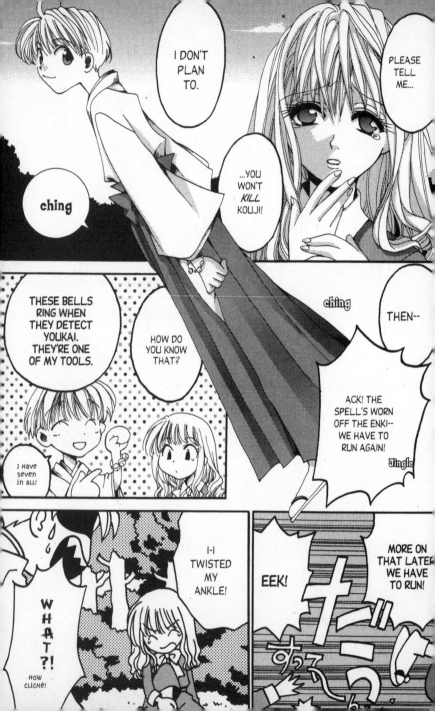

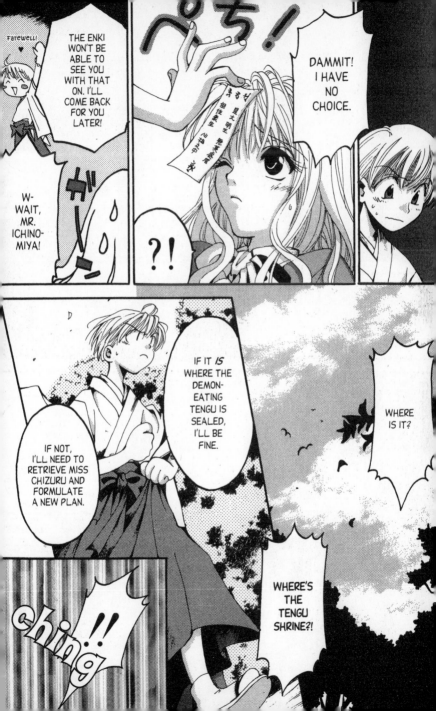

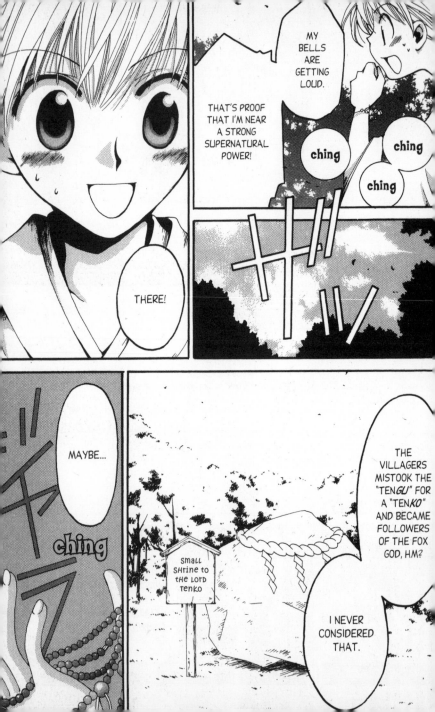

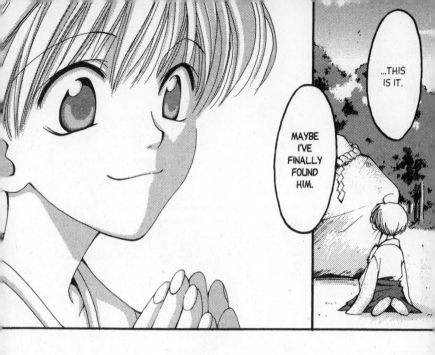

I'VE SCOURED THE EARTH FOR YOU, TENGU.

COME OUT AND BLOW MY MIND.

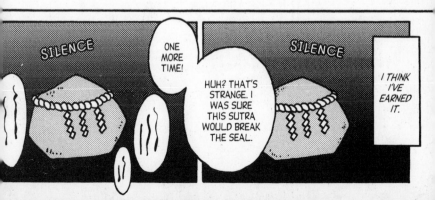

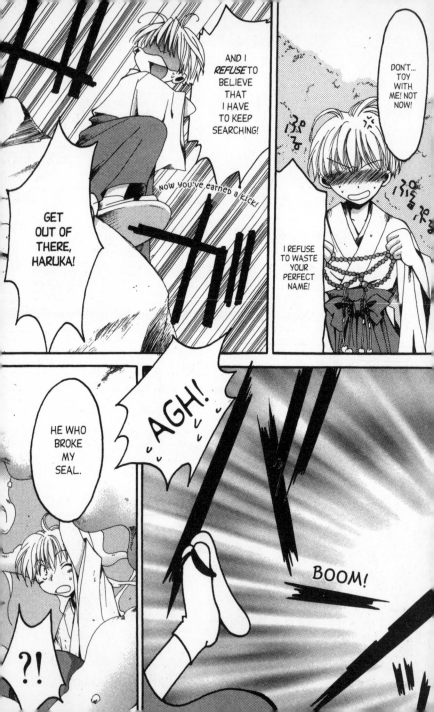

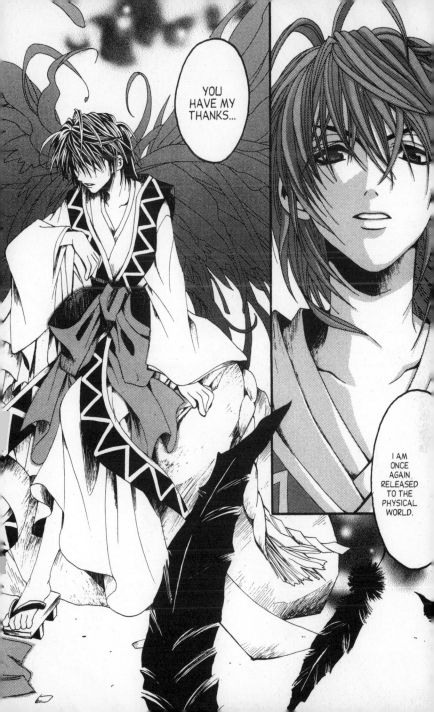

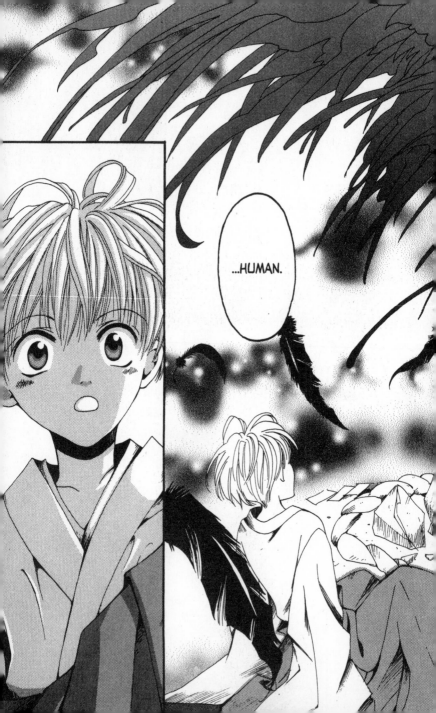

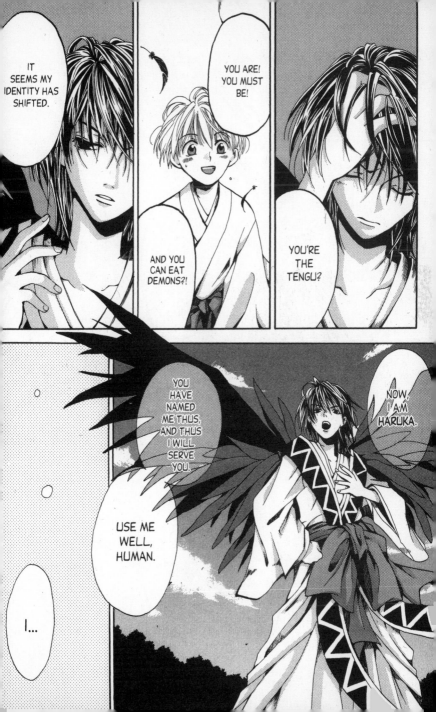

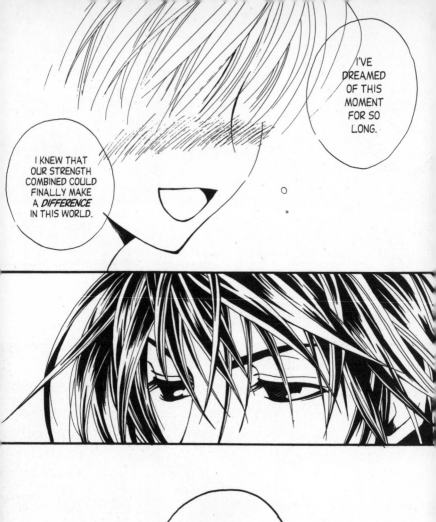

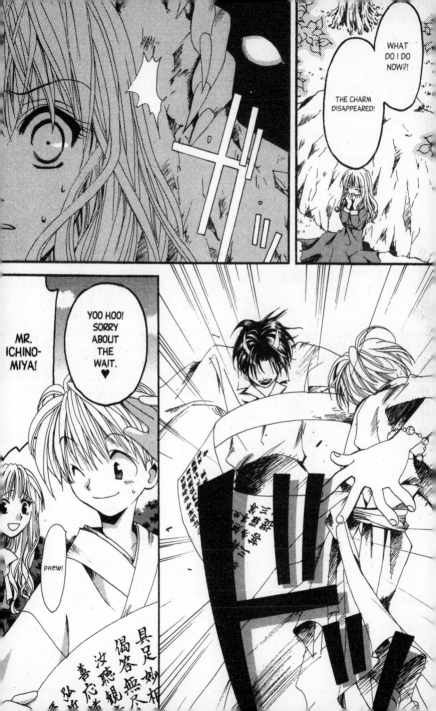

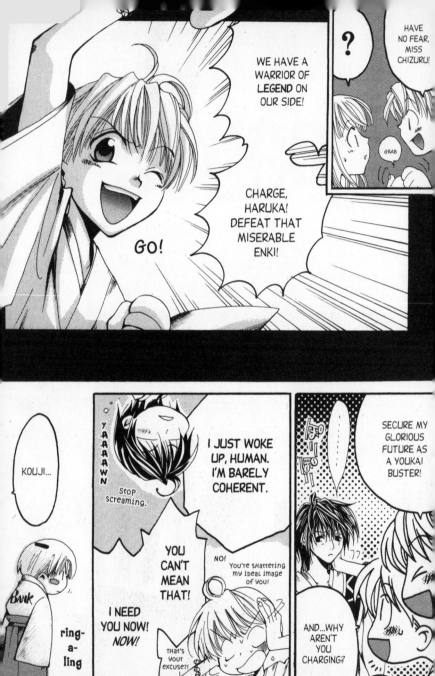